THE TRUTH ABOUT LYNCHING *and* THE NEGRO IN THE SOUTH

IN WHICH THE AUTHOR PLEADS THAT THE SOUTH BE MADE SAFE FOR THE WHITE RACE

BY

WINFIELD H. COLLINS, A.M., Ph.D.

AUTHOR OF

The Domestic Slave Trade of the Southern States

ISBN: 978-1-63923-758-6

Printed: February 2023

Published and Distributed By:
Lushena Books
607 Country Club Drive, Unit E
Bensenville, IL 60106
www.lushenabks.com

ISBN: 978-1-63923-758-6

TABLE OF CONTENTS

PREFACE

IN the preparation of these pages an effort has been made to discover and present the truth in regard to the Negro in the South. The first three chapters need not be considered an attempt at justification of lynching nor an effort at palliation of the disorder, but rather as a setting forth of the facts, conditions, and extenuating circumstances in such connection. The purpose of the other four chapters is to throw light upon the mental, moral, and material condition of the Negro.

W. H. C.

REIDS GROVE, MD.,
January 30, 1918.

The Truth About Lynching and the Negro in the South

CHAPTER I

THE LYNCHING OF NEGROES IN THE SOUTH PREVIOUS TO THE CIVIL WAR

I is generally supposed that the custom or practice of lynching in this country had its origin in the method of punishment used by a Virginian farmer named Lynch, who during the Revolutionary War sought in this way to maintain order in his community or section,—hence, Lynch's Law, and Lynch law, from which comes the word "lynching."

In the beginning, however, the term seldom, if ever, conveyed the meaning "to put to death"; nor does it appear that Negroes were lynched even so often as whites. The methods of punishment in the majority of cases consisted of riding the victim on a rail, beating or whipping him, and often of giving him a coat of tar and feathers.

Moreover, it does not appear that lynching in

any form was very common in the early history of the country. Indeed, in 1839 a writer in the *Southern Literary Messenger* [1] began a brief article on the subject with the following:

"Forty years ago the practice of wreaking private vengeance or of inflicting summary or illegal punishment for crime actual or pretended which has been glossed over by the name Lynch law was hardly known except in sparse, frontier settlements beyond the reach of courts and legal proceedings."

Newspapers, periodicals, and other literature of the time show,—as the years pass,—an interesting change in the meaning of the term Lynch law. As the practice of lynching increased, the methods of the executors of this law became more severe, and it grew more often to mean "a putting to death." Possibly the change in meaning was partly due to the fact that lynching came to be a favorite means of punishment for abolitionists, their Negro dupes, and for both Negroes and whites who might be found guilty of unusual or shocking crimes.

The change from the mild to the severer meaning of the term was gradual. From 1830 to 1840

[1] Vol. V, p. 218.

it seldom meant "to put to death"; from 1850 to 1860 it very often had that meaning, and by 1870, or 1875,—this became the almost exclusive interpretation of "lynching," even as at present.

The "New English Dictionary" defines Lynch law as "the practice of inflicting summary punishment upon an offender, by a self-constituted court armed with no legal authority; it is now limited to the summary execution of one charged with some flagrant offense." So this is about the sense (unless otherwise indicated) in   I shall use the expression "Lynch law," or "lynching," in these pages.

In seeking a cause for the great increase of lynching, whether in its milder or severer form, from about 1830, I think one need not hesitate to give first place to the Anti-Slavery agitation; and the Southampton Slave Insurrection is also to be considered as contributory.

When, about 1830, the Anti-Slavery agitation began to attract some attention there were a number of anti-slavery societies in the South. These, however, soon broke up as those formed in the North became unreasonable. The net effect of the societies in the North was to produce distrust and even hatred at the South. It could hardly have been otherwise, for the Northern anti-slavery propagandists during the whole period of such agitation seemed to have regard for neither law nor common sense. Nothing better could have been expected from them, however, as, for the most part, the abolitionists were poor, misguided men and women. Instead of adopting persuasive methods and of showing a fair and conciliatory spirit, they were dictatorial, inflammatory and menacing. And by whatever of higher law or Divine inspiration they may have claimed to be actuated, they failed to recognize the fact that they had to deal with human beings and human institutions.

Again, on whatever lofty plane of morality they professed to stand, their propaganda did not comprehend even ordinary honesty. Indeed, it appears as only another illustration,—for history affords so many instances,—of self-elected good men endeavoring to impose their own half-blind perception of the way of the Lord, or their own ideas of what constitutes righteousness on their open-eyed and superior fellow-men, and exerting themselves to the utmost of their ignorance in such efforts,—thus, as is usual in such cases, making hell on earth. Even the Kaiser claims to be the agent of the Lord.

William Lloyd Garrison, the leading exponent of the abolition movement, called the Constitution of the United States "An Agreement with

Death and a Covenant with Hell." In the beginning his most earnest supporters were some pious old women, who doubtless with fair intelligence and good intentions, like many professed good people, let their emotions aided by their imagination get the better of their heads. They seemed to enjoy criticizing the South, with the occasional diversion of holding prayer-meetings for Negroes.

However, it was a long while (even in the North) before the abolition movement gained much headway. Garrison himself was treated with scarcely more consideration in the North than awaited those Apostles of anti-slavery that should go South, having persuaded themselves that they were called to preach the "gospel" of abolition in that benighted section. Indeed, once, in 1835, he hid himself in order to escape from a mob of some thousands of people,—including many of the leading citizens of Boston,—that had collected in front of his office. Some of the crowd found him and soon had a rope around his neck, but he was rescued by the mayor of the city. About two years later, however, a noted abolition editor, Rev. E. P. Lovejoy, was killed by a mob in Illinois.

In 1856 *The Liberator* made the following remarkable statement in regard to the treatment of abolitionists in the South:

"A record of the cases of Lynch-Law in the Southern States reveals the startling fact that within twenty years over three hundred white persons have been murdered upon the occasion—in most cases unsupported by legal proof—of carrying among the slaveholders arguments addressed to their own intellects and consciences as to the morality and expediency of slavery."[2]

This is evidently a great exaggeration. If it were alleged that over three hundred had been "lynched," bearing in mind that during those years the word, more often than otherwise, meant giving the victim a coat of tar and feathers, and so on, it would not even then be in accord with what is indicated by better evidence. Books of travel and other literature of the time fail to show that any great number of abolitionists in the South met death by lynching during the period in question.

Indeed, a booklet, "The New Reign of Terror," published early in 1860,—and in all probability compiled by Garrison himself,—is weighty evidence against the truth of this statement. According to *The Liberator,* the booklet gave "multiplied newspaper accounts of lynchings, murders, and mob raids of the Black Power of the Slave States within the past year [1859]." Although

² *The Liberator,* Dec. 19, 1856.

this was a time of intense excitement throughout the South,—a time when a more bitter feeling was manifested against abolitionists than in any previous period, a careful examination of the "New Reign of Terror" failed to reveal more than one case in which an abolitionist was put to death by lynching.

There is much evidence of a law-abiding spirit in the South (especially in the eastern part) at the beginning of the Anti-Slavery agitation. Indeed, even when lynching was resorted to, it seems to have been done with great reluctance.

Another thing that had some effect on lynching was the Southampton Slave Insurrection, which occurred in 1831. About sixty white men, women, and children were murdered in cold blood by Negroes. However, not more than one of the fifty or more Negroes concerned in it was lynched. Instead, they were given a fair trial, and disposed of according to law. The Insurrection may have caused an increase in the lynching of Negroes by the fact that it begat a kind of fear and distrust of the blacks everywhere, caused them to be more carefully looked after, and more severely dealt with when refractory or guilty of crime.

This was no more than could be expected. In 1835 there were four great fires in the city of Charleston,—all supposed to have been the work of slaves. Moreover, up to 1860 there were rumors of insurrections, and many minor insurrections did take place. The abolitionists, not without reason, were accused of trying to set the slaves against their masters and of fostering outbreaks of the bondmen.

Such things could hardly be considered lightly, for in many places the whites were practically at the mercy of the Negroes. A quotation from Murray,[3] an English traveler, may be interesting as it gives an example of the situation in many of the Slave States:

"The farms of the two gentlemen whom I visited occupied the whole of the peninsula formed by the James River; they had each two overseers: thus (their families being young) the effective strength of white men on their estates amounted to six: the Negroes were in number about two hundred and fifty: nor was there a village or place within many miles from which help could be summoned."

Could one reasonably expect that any man so situated would be inclined to be too ceremonious with any person, black or white, however innocent or saintlike his looks, who might be caught tampering with the Negroes and thereby jeopardize

[3] Murray, "Travels in North America," Vol. I, p. 166.

the safety of his family and those of his neighbors as well? When one considers the exasperating circumstances, the wonder is not that there were so many lynchings but rather that there were so few, comparatively.

Some interesting lynchings occurred in 1835. They were widely commented upon at the time. One, the case of a mulatto from Pennsylvania, who was supposed to have some connection with the abolitionists, was burned at St. Louis for killing an officer who was trying to arrest him for some crime he had committed. The judge's charge to the grand jury in reference to the matter is worth consideration as it indicates the attitude toward lynching shown at the time by those in authority:

"He told the jury that a bad and lamentable deed had been committed in burning a man alive without trial, but that it was quite another question whether they were to take any notice of it. If it should prove to be the act of a few, every one of those few ought undoubtedly to be indicted and punished; but if it should be proved to be the act of the many, incited by that electric and metaphysical influence which occasionally carries on a multitude to do deeds above and beyond the law, it was no affair for the jury to interfere with."[4]

The same year, 1835, two Negroes were burned near Mobile.[5]   The circumstances were these:

Upon the failure of a certain little girl and her brother to return from school at the proper time a search was made and the body of the girl at last found.   It appeared that she had been violated, then murdered, and her body hid in order to conceal the crime.   Soon after this, two young ladies of Mobile were seized by two Negroes near the place where the body of the little girl was found. The young ladies escaped.   At once suspicion pointed to these Negroes as the murderers of the children.   They were arrested, tried by the court, and found guilty.   The gentlemen of Mobile, it is said, then seized the Negroes, took them to the place of their crime, and burned them.   For it was felt that the law did not furnish adequate means of punishment for such fiendish criminality.

Another noted instance of lynching took place at Vicksburg in the same year.   This time it was not a Negro but whites that were lynched.

For many years the population of the Mississippi Valley had been increasing rapidly.   The courts of law were so few, weak, or dilatory, that

[4] Harriett Martineau, "Retrospect of Western Travel," pp. 30-1.
[5] *Ibid.*, "Society in America," Vol. II, pp. 141-2.

the better citizens sometimes found it necessary to take the law into their own hands in order to insure for themselves protection. Such was the case at Vicksburg. Some gamblers had lately made this town their home and had established themselves at the low taverns to which they decoyed the young men of the vicinity. These, after being plundered and debauched, often cast their lot with the gamblers and became almost as desperate as their corrupters. After a while all restraint was thrown off, and the gamblers went about the streets even in the daytime armed with deadly weapons, and by their insults, drunkenness, and crimes, made themselves a terror to the inhabitants.

At length the people, having decided to put an end to such conditions, held a meeting and passed resolutions, giving the gamblers notice to leave within twenty-four hours. But, instead of doing so, they garrisoned themselves in a house. This the men of the town surrounded, and breaking open a door, they were fired upon from within, one of the most prominent men of the town being killed. This so enraged the people that they took the house by storm. Five of the gamblers were made prisoners. Then a procession, headed by the leading men of the town, led the gamblers to execution, hung them, and buried them together in a ditch.

Featherstonhaugh, an English traveler, in writing of the Mississippi gamblers, says:

"In various travels in almost every part of the world, I never saw such a collection of unblushing, low, degraded scoundrels."[6]

He also quotes a passage from a justification of the above lynching, which was drawn up by the people of Vicksburg, and is as follows:

"Society may be compared to the elements, which, although, 'order is their first law,' can sometimes be *justified only by a storm.* Whatever, therefore, *sickly sensibility or mawkish philanthropy* may say against the course pursued by us, we hope that our citizens *will not relax the code of punishment* which they have enacted against this infamous, unprincipled, and baleful class of society; and we invite Natchez, Jackson, Columbus, Warrenton, and all our sister towns throughout the State, in the name of our insulted laws, of offended virtue, and of slaughtered innocence, to aid us in exterminating this deep-rooted vice from our land. The *revolution* has been conducted here *by the most respectable* citizens, heads of families, *members* of *all classes and professions* and pur-

[6] G. W. Featherstonhaugh, "Excursion through the Slave States," pp. 136-9.

suits. None have been heard to utter a syllable of censure against either the act *or the manner in which it was performed;* and so far as we know, public opinion, both in town and country, is decidedly in favor of the course pursued. We have never known the public so unanimous on any subject."

Only a few days before the Vicksburg affair two white men and seven Negroes were lynched about forty miles from Vicksburg on the charge of attempting to organize an insurrection of slaves. Featherstonhaugh quotes the following account of it from a newspaper:

"Twenty miles from this place [Jackson, in Madison County] a company of white men and Negroes were detected before they did any mischief. On *Sunday* last they hung two steam doctors, one named Cotton and the other Saunders; also, seven Negroes without law or gospel, and from respectable authority we learn that there were *two preachers* and ten Negroes to be hanged this day."

That such lynchings were exceptional in the South before about 1855, or even before the war, is shown by the fact that these cases were mentioned by several different travelers and the papers of the time as well. I examined with more or less care books of travel too numerous to mention,— scores of them,—for the period between 1830 and 1860. Those travelers, especially, who visited the South between 1838 and 1854 are eloquently silent on the subject. I examined *The Liberator* [7] for 1839 and 1840, but found mention of only one Negro who was put to death by a mob. No State was given so I am not sure whether it was in the North or the South. However, it gave five instances of Negroes legally executed in the South; one for rape, one for arson, one for firing on two white men and threatening two others, and two for connection with an attempt at insurrection. Two more cases may be given: that of a Negro in New Orleans suspected of rape and murder, and one sentenced in Kentucky for rape upon two white women.

Again, a search of *The Liberator* for 1848 and 1849; Niles' *Register,* July, 1845-January, 1849; *The Vicksburg Sentinel,* and *The Augusta* (Va.) *Democrat,* July, 1846-January, 1849, reveal but two lynchings: One a Negro "hung by a committee of citizens" at Bentonville, Arkansas;

[7] In using *The Liberator* one needs to be careful, for the same instance is often found to be given two or three different times, —weeks, even months apart.

the other, a white man named Yeoman, in Florida, for robbery. The latter was given both by Niles' *Register* and a book of travel. However, one Negro was sentenced to death in the South for rape, and ten legally executed, the majority for murder.

As one might naturally expect, *The Liberator* for 1855 and 1856 shows several lynchings in the South. At least six Negroes were lynched in the South during these years,—two for rape (one of whom was burned) and four for murder (one of whom also was burned). Two of these criminals were lynched in Arkansas by a mob,—after being acquitted by the court,—led by the sons of their master, whom they had killed. Two white men were also lynched: one, in Texas, for stealing Negroes, and the other, in Missouri, for poisoning a spring. Moreover, eighteen Negroes were legally executed in the South: two for rape, and nearly all the others for murder. In addition, seven Negroes were mentioned as under sentence of death.

A quotation from Bancroft clearly shows that the number of lynchings in the South at this time hardly compares with the number in the West:

"Out of 535 homicides which occurred in California during the year 1855," he says, "there were but seven legal executions and forty-nine informal ones."[8]

One does not need to go far in order to find the causes of the increase of lynching in the South after 1850, or for the disorder and commotion both North and South as well.

In 1850 the Fugitive Slave law was passed. The endeavor to enforce it gave great impetus to the abolition cause. in the North; this reacted on the South. Indeed, many of the same men who were ready to hang Garrison in 1835, now became his earnest adherents. This great change in the feeling of the North opened the way for the enthusiastic reception of "Uncle Tom's Cabin" when, in 1852, it was published in book form. The author of this book ingeniously made the isolated and exceptional incidents of slavery appear as the general condition of the institution; however, as for the chief character of the book, Uncle Tom, it is very doubtful whether the pure Negro race ever produced such an individual. Nevertheless, this piece of fiction was read by hundreds of thousands both in the North and in foreign countries as if it were "Gospel truth."

Another thing that added to the excitement and helped the abolitionists was the Dred Scott Decis-

[8] H. H. Bancroft, "Popular Tribunals," Vol. I, p. 749.

ion, given in 1857. Then, in 1859, came "Helpers' Impending Crisis," a book of great influence. At last, in 1859, as if to "cap the climax," the whole country was startled by John Brown's Raid. After this, the greater part of the South, suddenly, became an extremely unhealthful place for both abolitionists and unruly, criminal, or insurrectionary Negroes.

"The New Reign of Terror," mentioned above, published early in 1860, not many months after John Brown's Raid, has the following, which indicates the then feeling in the South:

"In almost every city, town, and village south of the border slave-holding States, Vigilance Committees have been appointed to put to inquisition every Northern man who makes his appearance in the place, whether as foe or friend. Even harmless young women, who have gone from Northern boarding schools to be teachers of Southern children have been waited upon by respectable and even clerical gentlemen with the polite hint that the sooner they leave the State the better for their safety."

The Augusta Dispatch [9] warned the South against "strange loafing white men, and especially

[9] Quoted by *Liberator,* Aug. 24, 1860.

the one-horse invalid preachers from the North,"
for it said:

"We would guard well against imposition from
transient 'candles of the Lord' lest we suffer them
to light the fires of insurrection, instead of bearing
aloft the light of the Gospel."

Indeed, in many Southern States there were
rumors of Negro insurrections. In Mississippi,
Georgia, and Alabama plots of Negro insurrections were discovered in 1860. In Texas, however, the greatest excitement prevailed. What
was supposed to be a State-wide insurrection was
discovered. Dallas and other towns were partly
burned before it was checked.

The excited state of the public mind in some instances may have suspected plots of insurrection
when none existed. However that may be,
wherever and whenever such a plot was discovered, investigation nearly always pointed to the
abolitionists as the instigators. Indeed, even when
Negroes were insubordinate and refractory on a
plantation, it was often found that they had been
tampered with by abolitionists.

Occasionally, when such things were proved
against an abolitionist beyond the possibility of a
doubt, he would be immediately hanged to the

limb of some convenient tree. Several were so dealt with in connection with the insurrection in Texas. As a rule, however, when the proof was not so conclusive, a severe whipping, or a coat of tar and feathers, would be given him, and then he would be forcefully admonished to leave the South.

One cannot but reach the conclusion that the anti-slavery agitation was detrimental to the happiness and welfare of the slaves, and to the free Negroes as well. Of the latter there were in the slave States (by the fifties) something like 225,-000. The majority of these were indolent, miserable, and often vicious. Finally some States passed laws giving them the option of leaving such State or of being sold into slavery.

Nearly everywhere more stringent regulations and laws [10] were made both for slaves and for free Negroes. The slaves were deprived of many former privileges, the enjoyment of which by the Negroes might be dangerous for the white people. They were more closely guarded and much more harshly dealt with when guilty of offenses or crimes. Indeed, three Negroes in as many States were burned in 1859 for the murder of their mas-

[10] The attitude toward both slaves and free Negroes varied in different Southern States; but as a result of the anti-slavery agitation, as we approach 1860 the more severe it becomes.

ters,—one of these was burned before 1,500 or 2,000 people.

Nevertheless, it is quite evident that throughout the period from 1830 to 1860 the lynching of Negroes was sporadic,—and usually was resorted to only for exceptional reasons. Generally the law was allowed to take its course. However, it is also plain that after 1850 the law was relied on less and less, while the people more and more assumed the initiative in such matters as the excitement increased. What was true as regards the Negro was undoubtedly true also as regards the treatment of the abolitionists.

CHAPTER II

LYNCHING DURING THE CIVIL WAR AND THE CARPET-BAG RULE

IT is said that an Abolitionist Society by a bribe of $3,000 induced the slave valet of Henry Clay to leave him and go North. The Society thought that this large sum would be well spent in producing what would appear to be such a noteworthy example of dissatisfaction with the condition of slavery. Though the Negro accepted the money and left, he soon repented and returned to his master. Thereupon Clay gave him $3,000 (for the Negro had long since spent the bribe), telling him that when he had returned the sum to those who had tried to corrupt him that he would be restored to his master's service. The money was given back as directed and Clay then took the Negro back as his valet.

Such a case was, no doubt, exceptional. In one way or another, however, the abolitionists produced more or less dissatisfaction among the slaves and were almost wholly responsible for the escape to the North of something like an average of 2,000 a year. The Negroes did not always find conditions in the North so favorable as they had been led to suppose. As a consequence it did not infrequently happen that a "runaway" Negro would become dissatisfied and return of his own free will to his master in the South.

During the Civil War those slaves who for any reason had become dissatisfied with their condition embraced the first opportunity to gather in the wake of the Union army,—mainly, no doubt, to shun work.

While this was true as an exception, the great mass of the slaves remained quietly at work on the plantations. Thus, instead of creating antagonism between the two races, the War served rather to foster and cement a good feeling between them; indeed, throughout its darkest days they lived harmoniously side by side. Elizabeth Collins, an Englishwoman, who was in South Carolina the greater part of the War, says:

"In regard to the slave population of Charleston, I may say that they appear to be, almost without exception, happy and contented."[1]

Indeed, an examination of several Southern

[1] Elizabeth Collins, "Memories of the Southern States," p. 46.

newspapers and some books of travel [2] revealed but two possible cases of lynching of Negroes in the South during the War: A Mr. Harris, Uchee, Alabama, was murdered by six of his Negroes, whereupon:

"The citizens of the county about ninety in number, after consultation, determined upon the immediate execution of the murderers." [3]

The other case was in Mississippi: Some Negroes were hung, seemingly, for trying to get on a steamboat in order to escape from slavery.[4] *The Liberator* [5] mentions two instances of Negroes being lynched in New York in 1863: A negro in jail at Newburg, on suspicion of rape, was taken out by a mob "who pounded him almost to death and then hung him on a tree until he was finished." Two were also lynched in the City of New York, one of whom, it seems, was roasted alive.

In no place was there any mention of any Negroes being lynched for rape in the South during the War. Indeed, it is often said that during the

---

[2] *The Frankfort* (Ky.) *Commonwealth, The Charleston* (S. C.) *Mercury, The Louisville* (Ky.) *Democrat* for 1863 and 1864, *The Daily News* (Savannah), for 1862 and one Northern paper, *The Liberator* (Boston) for 1863. The books of travel include Elizabeth Collins' "Memories of the Southern States."

[3] Savannah *News,* June 9, 1862.

[4] *The Liberator,* Feb. 22, 1863.

[5] *Ibid.,* June 26 and July 24, 1863.

Civil War when the white men were nearly all away from home, leaving the white women almost at the mercy of the slaves, no Negro was guilty of a criminal outrage against them.[6] It may be true. Viewed in the light of the sporadic occurrence of the crime under the restraining influence of slavery before the War, and of its quite frequent occurrence sometime after, it is both remarkable and suggestive.

It may truly be regarded as evidence not only of the generally fair treatment that, according to unprejudiced travelers, they were receiving in slavery, as well as a tribute to their fidelity, but it also makes it obvious that the Negro and the Southern white man might have continued in harmony mutually advantageous after the War, had both been free from outside influences.

Almost immediately after the War, however, the South began to "swarm" with harebrained preachers and teachers from the North, ostensibly to elevate the Negro; as a rule, though, they served no better purpose than to aid in setting the Negro against his former master. For, it seems, they cared not what became of the white man so they secured the "salvation" of the Negro, entirely ignoring that saying of Scripture which is to the effect that those who fail to serve first their

⁶ Grimke, "Lynching of Negroes," p. 29.

own house or people have denied the faith and are ! worse than infidels.[7]

Such a condition of affairs was promoted by Congress, who, at about the close of the War established the so-called "Freedmen's Bureau," and shortly after passed the Civil Rights bill, both of which tended to cause friction between the two races. However, as compared with that of a few years later, the trouble does not appear to have been very serious notwithstanding exaggerated accounts which were reported to Northern papers. In most parts of the South and at most times for something like two years after the War, there was comparative quiet and safety.

The crimes of the Negroes during these years were for the most part of a trifling kind,—petty thievery and robbery. However, it is true they committed crimes of a very serious nature, also. Notwithstanding, the law was generally allowed to have its way. Harriett Martineau observes in one of her books that nothing struck her more than the patience of the slave-owners of the South with their slaves. Even during the first years after the War a patient and even indulgent spirit was often manifested by the leading whites toward the Negroes as to their shortcomings and sometimes it extended to their serious crimes.

[7] *I Timothy*, V, 8.

For instance, in 1866, near Rome, Georgia, a whole family consisting of a man, wife, and two daughters, were murdered, and one of the women, ravished. The newspaper account ends with:[8]

"It was difficult to restrain the people from inflicting summary punishment upon them."

For such a crime now, a Negro would likely be burned alive. The same paper quotes the following from *The Raleigh Progress:* [9]

"Charles Wethers, the rascally Negro, who attempted to commit a rape upon a highly respectable young lady of this county some weeks ago, was placed in the stocks this morning for the last time, having completed his sit still in the burning sun for two hours during each day of this week. He was returned to jail and will remain in the custody of the sheriff till the workhouse is ready, in which institution he will labor at five dollars per month until the fine, $200, and the cost of the trial have been liquidated by muscle."

Would it now be possible for any one to take such a tolerant, if not even good-natured,—view of such an affair?

[8] *Richmond Times,* Oct. 24, 1866.
[9] *Ibid.,* Sept. 11, 1866.

In order to make a comparison I have selected for study, here, two three-year periods: First, 1866-7-8, including the year before and year after the passing of the Reconstruction Act of 1867 for the South; second, 1873-4-5, when the carpet-bag rule, which resulted from the Reconstruction policy of Congress, was in full operation.   Although the number of lynchings during the first and second periods are in striking contrast, even this but faintly indicates the great change from the comparative tranquillity of the first (as illustrated by newspapers)[10] to the confusion, chaos, and crime of the second.

In 1866, one Negro was lynched in the South for attempted rape, another was sentenced to death for rape, and one was sentenced to the penitentiary for a like crime.   Also, near Smithfield, Ohio, Negroes committed outrages on two girls. In Kentucky three white men were lynched for murder, and three more were put to death by a

---

[10] Newspapers examined for first period: *Richmond Times,* 1866; *Richmond Times, Baltimore American,* and the *New Orleans Times,* 1867; and the *Sun* (Baltimore), *Leader* (Baltimore) and Atlanta *News Era,* 1868; second, *Missouri Republican, Baltimore American,* 1873; *Richmond Enquirer, Baltimore American, St. Louis Republican,* 1874; *Baltimore American, St. Louis Republican, Richmond Enquirer,* and *New Orleans Republican,* 1875.   I do not claim that I found every case of lynching in the South for either period, but as the same case would often be found in two or three different papers, I believe that I found practically all.

band of regulators. No doubt Kentucky was influenced in such matters by the example of the West.

The following occurred in 1867: one Negro lynched in Missouri by Germans for the murder of a German; a Negro given sixty lashes in Delaware for assaulting two white women; three Negroes legally hanged at Charleston, S. C., for outrage. In the North, two or more Negro soldiers, deserters, lynched in Kansas for the rape of a white woman; four white men lynched in Indiana for murder and robbery; thirty men hanged in three Kansas counties by Vigilantes during the winter and spring.

For 1868: Two Negroes who confessed to the horrible murder of a white family in Mississippi were taken from a sheriff by a band of Negroes and burned; [11] one Negro was lynched in Kentucky for rape and another in Maryland for attempted rape; two Negroes, in jail for murder, lynched in Mississippi after boasting that the *Loyal League* would prevent their execution, even if convicted; a man lynched in Tennessee after he

[11] This lynching of the two Negroes by Negroes is the only case I found where Negroes alone did the lynching in cases of crime against the whites. Several times during the seventies, however, Negroes are found helping the whites to lynch some Negro guilty of crime. It shows, I believe, that in some places, at least, the Negroes were yet in accord with the Southern whites.

had confessed to the murder of three men at different times. In North Carolina over thirty Negro desperadoes, who confessed to several murders and robberies, were captured and put in jail. Ten Adam's Express robbers were lynched in Indiana; two men lynched for murder in Illinois and one for stealing horses in Colorado.[12]

In 1873, however, six Negroes were lynched in the South for rape; three were legally executed for the same crime; one, condemned to be hung, and three awaiting trial—in all, thirteen Negroes charged with rape. In Louisiana, three Negroes were lynched in the presence of 1,000 people for an atrocious murder; four men were also lynched in Louisiana for cattle-stealing, and another in the same State for arson. Also, one white man was lynched in Tennessee by fifteen Negroes. Two Negroes were legally hanged for murder,—one in Kentucky, the other in Virginia. In the North: One white man was lynched in Ohio for rape; a Negro and a white man were lynched in Nebraska for robbery, also a Negro for murder; two men were lynched in Montana for murder and two in Kansas for supposed murder.

During the year 1874, eleven Negroes and one

[12] So far as the North and West are concerned, I simply happened to find such without any special search. I was searching carefully for lynchings in the South, etc.

white man were lynched in the South for rape, while two Negroes were legally executed for the crime. In two instances,—one in Arkansas, the other in Missouri,—both Negroes and whites took part in lynching Negroes. Three Negroes were also lynched in the South for murder and two for riot; and four Negroes in Tennessee for threatening to kill some whites and to sack and burn a town. In addition, ten white men were lynched, four in Arkansas and one in Missouri for horse-stealing, the others in the States of the Southwest for scandalous murders. In the North, two Negroes were lynched for murder, and two Negroes in Pennsylvania and one white man in Kansas for rape. In the North, also, seven white men, one Mexican and one Chinaman were lynched for murder, and one white man for horse-stealing and another for thievery.

In 1875, the last year of the second period,—nine Negroes were lynched in the South for rape and four for attempted rape; also, one Negro guilty of rape, and another who attempted rape, escaped,—in all, fifteen rape cases.[13] One man and two Negroes were lynched for murder. Also one Negro was legally executed for rape, eleven

[13] In 1875, there was another interesting case in which both Negroes and whites, about equal in number, lynched a Negro for attempted rape of a white woman.

for murder, and one case cause not given. In the North, one Negro was lynched, cause not given, and one Negro guilty of rape, escaped. Three men, also, were lynched for murder, one for arson, and one in New York for robbery.

By comparing the two three-year periods it will be found that during 1866-8 there were seven cases of rape or attempted rape by Negroes in the South. In three instances they were lynched and in four, the law was allowed to take its course. While for 1873-5, twenty-six Negroes were lynched for rape, and four for attempted rape. Six Negroes were legally executed for rape, one was under sentence of death for the crime, three were awaiting trial and two escaped—in all forty-two Negroes in the South were charged with rape during the second period. This was just six times as many as for the first period. Further, ten times the number of Negroes were lynched for rape in the South during 1873-5 as during 1866-8, or but 43 — per cent of those charged with the crime during the first period as against 73 + per cent for the second.

That this wonderful change was due almost wholly to misgovernment at Washington, no one can doubt. Surely, History was never obliged to record a more colossal blunder in statesmanship than that of Congressional Reconstruction. Nor is it likely that any civilized people were ever before called upon to endure a system of misrule and legalized plunder equal to that which such legislation, maybe unwittingly, paved the way for inaugurating at the South.

The confusion, turmoil, and strife that it created is only too well known. Not only did it result in a cleavage of the social structure, setting one part against the other, but it also caused as much or more financial damage to the South than the War itself. For instance, four and one-half years of Reconstruction, it is said, cost the State of Louisiana alone over $106,000,000; while the assessed valuation of property in New Orleans dropped from $147,000,000 to $88,500,000 during eight years of carpet-bag rule.

It was made easy for political-fortune hunters from the North, with little concern for the good of either the whites or the blacks of the South, to gain position and power through cultivating the friendship of the ignorant, credulous, newly enfranchised Negroes. This they assiduously did from the start. At the same time they left nothing undone which might create and foster among the Negroes a feeling of ill will against and distrust of the Southern whites. If their former masters came into power, the Negroes were sometimes told, they would be reduced to slavery. The

Negroes' love of display was appealed to by encouraging them to form secret societies, to make public parades, and hold celebrations which tended to create a race consciousness and race solidarity. This, of course, was for the purpose of helping the carpet-baggers in perpetuating their power. If one considers the conditions, what else could be expected but riots and lynchings?

If the control of the Negroes in slavery times, with all the advantages to such end embodied in the institution of slavery, had often been one of anxiety to the South, how fearful must have been the conditions now that they were not only free from such control but enfranchised and taught by their new friends to be self-assertive, even if not sometimes encouraged in acts of violence against the Southern white people? It does, indeed, seem that a great part of the Negroes almost ran wild—for they were free, but did not understand how to use their freedom. So, lazy, worthless, robbing, murdering gangs of them went prowling through the South. For it is as natural for the Negro to sit in idleness, or shoot crap, to go on marauding expeditions or connive at insurrections, as it is for the white man to establish courts, collect libraries, and found schools.

Can History prove that the Negro, during his thousands of years of contact with superior races, has ever yet risen to the dignity of stable and progressive self-government? Even Liberia, with all the help that has been given her, is gradually sinking to the level of the surrounding barbarism. And what of San Domingo? Indeed, everywhere the tendency of the pure Negro is to fall when the white man's props are removed.

To return: If there ever was a time when the best elements in a society were justified in taking the law into their own hands, that time was during carpet-bag rule. The wonder now is that such a people as those of the South should have acted with even the moderation that appears.

That some of the carpet-bag governments were absolutely corrupt goes without saying. "Get all you can in any way you can" seemed to be the idea. Justice was for sale. In some instances, it is said, the criminal elements knew that any one could commit crime and escape punishment for a money consideration. A few examples may be of interest: [14] A man who was accused of outrageously murdering a woman, although caught and imprisoned, was released, it is said, without even a trial, for $800. Moreover, a Negro who had been sentenced by a court to the penitentiary was released and returned home on the same train as the sheriff who took him there. Indeed, the ac-

[14] *St. Louis Republican*, Sept. 14, 1875.

cusation was made that a certain carpet-bag governor, in order to help the Republican Party, connived at the killing of a number of Negroes in such a way that the blame might fall on the Southern whites.   At one place,[15] a court in passing judgment on a convicted Negro rapist merely sent him to the penitentiary, which so enraged the people of the community that they took him from jail and hanged him near the place of his crime.

In order that one may the better understand the reason for the development of the lynching spirit in the South the following quotations are given:

I.   "New Iberia, La., Sept. 13, the Parish of Vermillon for years has been infested with cattle thieves.   The people have been unable to obtain redress by process of law and last month they organized a vigilant committee as a last resort.   A large number of thieves and their confederates were given notice to leave within a specified time but instead of doing so armed themselves and threatened to destroy the town of Abbeville.   The Vigilantes pressed them and they scattered.   It is reported that three of the band were hung on Friday. . . . All kinds of vague rumors are afloat concerning the number executed." [16]

[15] *St. Louis Republican,* July 22, 1875.
[16] *Missouri Republican,* Sept. 14, 1873.

II.   "The right of a robbed people to revolt
against robbery. . . . In Edgefield, S. C., a few
days ago the country was startled by a resolution
adopted at a meeting of the citizens of the county,
which declared that, 'Parties black or white who
may be caught in the act of firing any house in this
county shall be dealt with in accordance with the
precedents of Lynch law, which is a part of the
unwritten law of America.'

"Edgefield people present a statement of facts
which while not justifying resort to Lynch law
shows a strong provocation for it.   Just before
the November election, the most prominent *white
Radical* of the county is said to have advised the
Negroes to burn the houses of the whites; and that
this advice was not lost on them seems to be
proved by the fact that thirteen citizens were
burned out of their homes by incendiaries between
the 7th and 19th of December.   The Radicals
have a large majority and they have used their
power without mercy.

"No security for persons or property, for the
Negroes and poor whites who act with them had
a majority on every jury so that it was impossible
to convict one of their number no matter how plain
the evidence.   And even if convicted was prompt-
ly pardoned by the infamous executive, Moses.
To such an extent was this carried that Carpenter,

the Republican Judge of the circuit, announced that he would not permit the State to be put to the expense of trying criminals who were pardoned as soon as convicted. The citizens assert that Lynch law is the only remedy for the evils they endure and therefore they proclaim it. They may be wrong but they are more sinned against than. sinning." [17]

III. "Augusta, Ga., Aug. 23.—Several prominent Negroes connected with the troubles in the counties below have made confessions. Jake Moorman, First Lieutenant of a Negro company, testifies on oath that 19 counties were to be embraced in the insurrection. All white men and ugly white women were to be killed. Pretty white women were to be spared and the land and spoils were to be divided among the Negroes.[18] All who have so far confessed testify to substantially the same as Jake Moorman." [19]

[17] Editorial, *St. Louis Republican*, Jan. 1, 1875.

[18] This recalls an account of the Texan Negro insurrection of 1860 as quoted by *The Liberator* of July 21, 1860: "The old females were to be slaughtered along with the men, and the young and handsome women were to be parcelled out among those infamous scoundrels. They had even gone so far as to designate their choice. . . . The Negroes have been incited to these infernal proceedings by the abolitionists."

[19] *St. Louis Republican*, Aug. 24, 1875. Accounts of riots in Mississippi, in which several were killed, were given by the same paper, Sept. 5, 7, 1875.

However, in some States,—for instance, Virginia, Maryland, and Delaware,—where the Southern whites had control, order was preserved and comparative quiet prevailed, while the lynching of Negroes was sporadic, not only during this early period, but even until the present. Discord and collisions between the two races have been almost unknown.

It is doubtful if any greater mistake was made in dealing with the South after the War than in disfranchising the leading Southern whites and granting the Negro suffrage. The Negro might have been given the ballot gradually as he proved himself fitted for it without any detriment. But considering the race as a whole—it may be putting it too mild—it may be too great a compliment to the Negro,—too disparaging to the intelligence of the average white boy,—to say that the Negroes, with some exceptions, at that time were no more fit for the ballot than seven-year-old boys. Nor was it any more reasonable to expect them to act the part of men in using it, or in political affairs, than to expect it from seven-year-old boys. They were, and to a large extent are yet, a race in its childhood.

President Lincoln, however, seems to have understood better than any one else of his party what was for the best interest of both races: That the Negroes, at least, for a while, with proper guarantees and restrictions, should be in a position of tutelage or apprenticeship to the whites. Indeed, there is little doubt that he expected the Southern States to make some such temporary arrangements, for in a proclamation, December 8, 1863, in reference to the reëstablishment of State governments by several States of the farther South, he says:

"That any provision which may be adopted by such State government, in relation to the freed people of such State which shall recognize and declare their permanent freedom, provide for their education, and which may yet be consistent as a temporary arrangement with their present condition as a laboring, landless and homeless class, will not be objected to by the National Executive."

But unfortunately for both races in the South, Lincoln was assassinated.

CHAPTER III

LYNCHING FROM THE END OF CARPET-BAG RULE TO THE PRESENT TIME

BEGINNING in 1885, *The Chicago Daily Tribune* [1] has kept a record of lynchings to the present time. Although statistics are to many very dry reading, nevertheless, to others, who are more impressed by facts than fancy, they are of the most intense interest. However that may be, here they

[1] Lynchings in the country for the past thirty-two years according to *The Chicago Daily Tribune*, Dec. 30, 1916:

1885	184	1901	130
1886	138	1902	96
1887	122	1903	104
1888	142	1904	87
1889	176	1905	60
1890	127	1906	60
1891	191	1907	65
1892	205	1908	100
1893	200	1909	87
1894	190	1910	74
1895	171	1911	71
1896	131	1912	64
1897	106	1913	48
1898	127	1914	54
1899	107	1915	98
1900	115	1916	58

appear to be indispensable to any satisfactory consideration of the subject.

The following statistics which are based upon the records of *The Chicago Daily Tribune* are compiled by periods: excepting the last which is for four years, these periods were taken almost indiscriminately for two years together, beginning with 1885 and 1886:

LYNCHINGS AND LEGAL EXECUTIONS FOR 1885 AND 1886

In the United States there were 314: 159 whites, 149 Negroes, and 6 Chinamen; 62 in the North, 252 in the South. Of those lynched in the South, 144 were Negroes; nearly all the whites were lynched in the Southwest for horse-stealing and murder; the Negroes were lynched for the following causes: 51, *rape;* 65, murder; 12, incendiarism; 6, arson; 3, cattle and horse-stealing; 1, self-defense; 1, robbery; 1, threat of political exposures; 1, assault; 2 cutting levees; 1, cause not mentioned. There were also 191 legal executions in the country; 72 Negroes in the South, 63 for murder and 9 for rape.

LYNCHINGS AND LEGAL EXECUTIONS FOR THE YEARS 1892 AND 1893

The whole number for the country was 436: 309 Negroes, 110 whites, 5 Mexicans, and 8 Indians. 53 lynchings in the North. 287 Negroes in the South: 74, rape; 18, attempted rape; 5, alleged rape; 1, attempted rape—*total, 88 for rape.* 99, murder. Nearly all the remainder for murderous assault, alleged or complicity in murder, arson, etc. 231 legal executions. 127 of these were Negroes in the South: 118, murder; 6, *rape;* 3, arson. In the North, 9 Negroes were legally executed for murder.

LYNCHINGS AND LEGAL EXECUTIONS FOR 1901 AND 1902

Lynchings for the country, 231. 29, North; 202, South. 194 Negroes; 35 whites; 2 Indians; 1 Chinaman. 185 Negroes lynched in the South: 40, rape; 19, attempted rape—*total, 59 for rape;* 63, murder; 7, murderous assault; 4, complicity in murder; 3, suspected murder; 3, implicated in murder; 2, sheltering murderers; 1, attempted murder; 6, theft; 5, Negroes' quarrel of profit sharing; 4, race prejudice; 1, making threats; 1, lawlessness; 1, mistaken identity; remainder, causes not given. In the North, 9 Negroes were lynched, 5 for rape and 4 for murder. There were 262 legal executions, of which 162 were Negroes. Execution of Negroes in South: 128, murder; 14, *rape;* 4, attempted rape. In the North, 16 Negroes were executed for murder, nearly all in Pennsylvania.

LYNCHINGS AND LEGAL EXECUTIONS FOR 1906 AND 1907

For the United States, 132. 3, North; 129, South. Negroes lynched in the South, 129: 27, rape; 25, attempted rape; 2 rape and murder; 1, suspected rape—*total, 55 for rape;* [2] 32, murder; 13, murderous assault; 5, race riot; remainder, minor causes. There were also 189 legal executions. Of these 115 were Negroes in the South,— 15 *for rape* and 100 for murder.

LYNCHINGS AND LEGAL EXECUTIONS FOR 1911-1914, INCLUSIVE

During these four years there were 235 lynchings in the United States. 11, North; 224, South.

[2] It seems fair to count rape, alleged rape, attempted rape, and so on,—all as rape; for it often happens that a Negro commits rape and escapes entirely. As an example, see account of the lynching of Ed. Berry (*Baltimore Sun,* Aug. 27, 1915). Berry confessed to twelve cases of criminal assault, each victim being a white woman.

In the North, 5 Negroes and 6 whites were lynched; in the South, 215 Negroes, 8 whites, and 1 Mexican. The causes for the lynching of Negroes in the South were as follows: 33, rape; 8, attempted rape; 2, alleged rape,—*total, 43 for rape;* 117, murder; 14, murderous assault; 3, complicity in murder; 1, suspicion of murder; 1, alleged murder; 5, arson; 5, race prejudice; 8, insulting white women; 11, by night riders in Kentucky; 1, refusal to pay note; 1, race troubles; 1, threat to kill; 1, assault and robbery; 1, horse-stealing; 1, annoying white women; remainder, cause not given. The number of legal executions in the whole country for the four years, were 381. Of these 136 were Negroes, 112 in the South, and 24 for murder in the North. In the South: 93, murder; 10, *rape;* 2, *attempted rape;* 1, burglary; 4, cause not given.

Now, adverting to the statistics for 1873-5,—not far removed from the beginning of the Negro-lynching disorder,—it is found that of the 44 Negroes lynched in the South during the three years, 30, or 70— per cent, were lynched for rape; while but 14, or 30+ per cent, were lynched for all other causes combined. Thus it is seen that at this time rape was practically the only cause for the lynching of Negroes in the South.

Moreover, it is quite evident from the statistics above given, beginning with 1885, that rape has continued to be, if not the whole cause for the lynching of Negroes in the South, anyhow almost that, with other crimes as merely incidental:

The three pairs of years,—1885-6, 1901-2, and 1906-7,—show 165 Negroes lynched in the South for rape, 160 for murder, and 127 for all other causes. Here rape takes the lead. Adding to these figures the statistics for 1892-3, the numbers for the four pairs of year are: 259, murder; 253, rape; and 227, minor causes. Again, adding for the four years 1911-14, the result for the twelve years, is: 376, or 39+ per cent, murder; 296, or 31+ per cent, rape; and 282, or 29+ per cent, minor causes. This would seem to indicate that rape was not even the leading cause.

However, according to the statistics for the twelve years under consideration, 502, or 57+ per cent of the Negroes in the South who committed murder during these years were legally executed, and but 376, or 43— per cent were lynched; while for rape, only 60, or 16+ per cent were legally executed, and 296, or 84— per cent were lynched.[3] The proportion may be stated thus:

[3] This argument assumes, of course, that all Negroes who murdered whites in the South were either lynched or legally executed, and that all Negroes caught who committed rape against white women were likewise dealt with. It seems to be about as fair in one case as the other to assume this.

$57:43::16:84=7+$. This shows that a Negro is more than seven times as liable to be lynched in the South for rape than even for murder.

Indeed, the belief of the average white man of the South that lynching is the most effective way of dealing with the Negro for his crime against white women also seems to be borne out by the statistics: In 1892-3, 88 Negroes were lynched for rape; in 1901-2, 59; while for the four years 1911-14, only 43. That this great reduction in rape cases and lynchings was not due to legal executions is shown by the fact that during the same time but 36 Negroes were legally executed, only 12 of these being for the four years 1911-14. Thus as a consequence of a reduction in the crime of rape by Negroes is noted a great reduction in the lynching of Negroes,—from 287 in 1892-3; 185, 1901-2; 129, 1906-7; to 91 for 1913-14.

However, during 1915 and 1916, 104 Negroes were lynched in the South as compared with 91 for 1913 and 1914. The increased number lynched for rape is very marked: being only 13 for 1913 and 1914, but twice the number, or 26, for 1915 and 1916. During the former two years, also, 6 Negroes were legally hanged for rape as compared to 12 for the latter. The proportion remains the same: thus during 1913 and

1914, 19 Negroes in the South were put to death for rape as compared with 38 for 1915 and 1916.

Although the legal execution of 12 Negroes in the South for rape during 1915 and 1916 may show a tendency to allow the law to take its course in such cases, may not the above statistics also indicate that when for a few years but few lynchings occurred, especially for the crime of rape, that the effect of such immediate and fearful punishment—consisting of burning as it sometimes does—gradually fades from the mind of the Negro inclined to such crime, with a great increase of rape as a consequence?

Again, in extenuation of lynching, it is important to observe, that, as a result of most crimes against the body, such as murder, but little, if any, humiliation attaches. But it is quite different in rape cases. Not only is there often great physical injury, but also an unutterable humiliation. Our civilization teaches that one should hold certain personal rights and considerations even more dear than life itself. To have in mind such ideas and live up to them measures our reach above lower peoples. That this feeling or spirit should be encouraged, rather than risk its check, is not to be questioned. Therefore, the average Southern white man does not believe that the innocent rape victim of a Negro should be obliged to endure further humiliation incident upon her appearance in a court of law.

In this connection, a set of resolutions published by those who lynched a Negro at Annapolis, Md., in 1875, are interesting. These resolutions, which set forth the causes of the act, were drawn up before the lynching took place and show serious consideration. I quote:[4]

"Fellow Citizens: In view of the fact that we are about to take into our hands the sword of justice to do to death one who is now incarcerated in our county jail, it is meet that we should give some reason for the purpose we hope to consummate. First, then: While we can but honor the deep feeling of interest manifested by those who are the proper guardians of our lives, our property, and our honor; and while we, as true and loyal citizens of the State of Maryland, and of Anne Arundel County, do bend to the supreme majesty of the law and acknowledge trials by jury as the very arch-stone in the grand edifice of human rights, still we know the vilest criminal is accorded the same rights under the law that belong to the petty thief, nor can this devil incarnate, should he claim his rights, be denied the privilege of a change of venue, such a circumstance might

[4] *Baltimore American,* June 15, 1875.

probably rob the gallows of its due and foil the
aims of the law. Before God we believe in the
existence of a higher code than that which is digni-
fied by the great seal of a Commonwealth and that
the high and holy time to exercise it is when the
chastity of our women is tarnished by the foul
breath of an imp from hell and the sanctity of our
homes invaded by a demon.

"Secondly, admitting that in the event of a
trial by a jury he shall be hanged—a highly probable result—yet would his execution be as illegal
as though done by a band of wronged citizens;
for must not a juror be a peer, and with a mind
free of bias, and where can a man be found com-
petent to try this case? Who can be found of
his level, and who that has heard has not already
convicted him in his mind? At best, that which
would be done under the semblance of law would
be a *more sham* by force of all the circumstances
connected with this horrible deed, and if under the
law the penalty is death, and we know the deed
was committed by him—we claim that there is no
moral difference in the means of destroying him,
and we act upon this conviction.

"Thirdly, we are not willing that the victim
shall be dragged into court to tell over and over
again the story of her terrible wrongs, or that
her name shall be entered upon the records of

our criminal jurisprudence for future reference."

Further comment on this lynching is unnecessary—unless indirectly: the Negro, child of Africa, but lately removed from the jungle, because of the necessity of the habitat of his origin, has had developed in him by nature, possibly, stronger sexual passion than is to be found in any other race.[5]   But he is infinitely lacking in the high mental, moral, and emotional qualities that are especially characteristic of the Anglo-Saxon, and it is a grievous mistake to attribute such high qualities to him.   When proper restraint is removed from the Negro he gets beyond bounds. The Anglo-Saxon, indeed, or members of that race, has a way of meeting extraordinary conditions with extraordinary means—hence lynching in order to hold in check the Negro in the South.

Indeed, a country occupied by two races so widely apart in origin, characteristics, and development as the whites and the Negroes of the Southern States—one race of the highest mental endowments and culture, the other of the lowest— one having a civilization that reaches back hundreds, if not thousands, of years, the other in the early dawn of civilization—might reasonably have two codes of law suited, as nearly as possible, to each race, respectively.

·[5] To make up for the high death rate.

A mode of punishment that would be out of place as to the white man may be well suited to the Negro.   Small-pox is not to be treated as chicken-pox.   Barbarous criminals require barbarous laws.   The innocent and law-abiding citizens of a State have rights as well as the criminals—at least, the right to protection from the criminals.   But let some crafty scoundrel finally get in jail, and he will be flooded with letters of consolation and sympathy from sentimental women and soft-headed men.[6]   And let some Negro brute, guilty of rape, suffer the punishment he so richly deserved at the hands of an outraged community, and one would think, if he considered the bitter censure from distant quarters, that the foundations of the government were being undermined, or that a poor lamb was set upon by a pack of howling wolves, thirsting for its blood, but not a word of commiseration for the family, or the victim, of the fiendish Negro's unbridled bestiality.

Moreover, instead of a Negro's being over-awed by the solemn deliberations of a court, rather, as he is the center of interest, he all but

---

[6] Joliet, Ill., Sept. 10 (1917), *Riot in State Prison.*   Rioters numbered about fifty.   Had become angered at impositions of restrictions.   "Among the privileges previously enjoyed by the convicts was an almost unlimited correspondence with sentimental women."—*Washington* (D. C.) *Star,* Sept. 10, 1917.

enjoys it.   For once in his life he finds himself in a position of prominence.   It would be contrary to the Negro nature if he were not somewhat elated at being the object of so much attention. Even were this not the case, he has no such appreciation of his degradation as the white man feels under similar circumstances.   Indeed, it would sometimes appear as almost a triumphal procession for him from the time he gets in jail until he reaches the gallows.   The two quotations below may help to justify this idea:

"Joe Clark, colored, . . . was hanged at this place on Friday forenoon, in the presence of about 3,000 persons, mostly Negroes.   Clark spoke about fifteen minutes, giving a detailed account of the murder and fully confessing the crime.   He advised all present to live an upright life. . . .   After he had shaken hands with his friends the trap was sprung, and thus the sentence of the court was duly executed.   Clark's last request was that the *black cap be kept off, so that all might see how easy he could meet death.*"[7]

The second one is taken from accounts of the execution at Denton, Md., of "Wish" Shepperd, colored, for the outrage of a fifteen-year-old white girl:[8]

[7] Taken from *Richmond Enquirer*, May 4, 1775.
[8] *Baltimore Sun*, August 27-28, 1915.

"He told his spiritual advisers that he had a message for the public: 'Tell all the young men to avoid the fate that awaits me by joining the church and attending its services.' [Evidently inspired by his preacher advisers] . . . He slumbered soundly, the guards noticed, and awoke early this morning apparently indifferent to his doom. . . . With a firm step he accompanied the officers and his spiritual advisers to the scaffold which was erected near the Choptank River. Passing *undismayed* through the throng which had gathered along the way from the prison *to the gallows. His gaze* passed fearlessly around surveying the people." . . .

Again, in connection with the lynching of Negroes in the South, one must not lose sight of the conditions that are peculiar to that section. The greater the number of Negroes in proportion to the whites in any State or community the easier it is for the Negro to commit crime and escape. And the Negro criminal does often escape. Seldom is it found that the Negro will aid in the detection of the Negro criminal, rather otherwise. Even the hope of escape is a wonderful encouragement to the criminally inclined.

Now, before the War, as is well known, the South was almost entirely an agricultural section.

It had but few cities and these were small. In the last thirty or forty years, however, it has been rapidly developing manufacturing industries. Some of the cities have become great industrial centers.

Nor is manufacturing confined at all to the large cities. Indeed, almost every town in some parts has a cotton mill or other establishment. As illustrations, I may mention Hickory, N. C., and La Grange, Ga. Hickory, with a population of about 5,000, has two large cotton mills; the Piedmont Wagon Shops, which employs hundreds of men; several furniture factories, saw mills, and other industrial interests. La Grange, a city of about 6,000, has ten cotton mills, one of which is valued at $1,000,000, and four of the others at $500,000, each. In the manufacture of cotton alone the South has increased from 316,000 bales in 1885 to 3,193,000 bales in 1915.

As a consequence the white people have largely been drawn to the towns and cities: the wealthier own and control the various business interests while the poorer ones contribute their help or labor. Few Negroes work in the factories, for the Negro seems to lack the qualities necessary: namely, punctuality, dependability, and a certain amount of mental alertness. So, in some parts of the South the whites are nearly all living in the towns and cities, while the country districts are filled with Negroes. However, even in such places there are some whites in the country, and as is evident, in additional danger.

Moreover, the population of several Southern States is nearly half Negro, while in two,—South Carolina and Mississippi,—it is even more than half Negro, being 55+ per cent and 56+ per cent, respectively. Indeed, in 53 counties of the South the Negro population of each exceeds 75 per cent. In Tensas Parish, La., and Isoquena County, Miss., the Negro population is 91.5 per cent and 94.2 per cent, respectively. That is, in every 1,000 persons one meets in Isoquena County, Miss., 942 are Negroes and but 58, white. Such conditions should be readily appreciated. Is it any wonder that the white man thinks it necessary to strike terror into the soul of the possible or incipient Negro criminal by any method that may cause him to stand in fear of an immediate and dreadful death?

Further, the origin of a great part of these Negroes, especially those of the farther South, is, also, worthy of consideration.

During the operation of the internal slave trade, it was usually the most undesirable, unruly, and the criminally inclined Negroes of the border slave States that were sold to the States of the farther South; nor should it be forgotten that between 1808 and 1860 the farther South received around 270,000 Negroes from outside the United States.[9]   It seems likely that the greater part of these were barbarous Negroes, directly from Africa.   It was these criminal and barbarous Negroes, along with their children and grand-children, who by the fortune of war, without home or master, were turned loose on the South.

Thus it is that the white woman is obliged to be constantly on her guard against the Negro,—otherwise rape cases would be multiplied.[10]   An idea of the necessity of this and the hardship of it may be had from the following quotation:

"In a population about evenly divided in North Carolina was a family of unpretending intelligent people.

"There was a school house only a mile and a half away, but they could not let their two daughters go to it.   They could not let them stir away from home unprotected.   They had to pay for their education at home, while at the same time they were being taxed for the education of the Negro children of the district.

[9] W. H. Collins, "The Domestic Slave Trade," p. 20.
[10] It is unlikely that all rape cases get in the papers. An intelligent resident of Rapides Parish, La., told the writer that four cases of rape occurred in that parish once within a month.

" 'Do you think,' was asked a leading Negro educator, 'that those girls could safely have gone to school?'

" 'It would depend upon the district,' was the reply. 'In some districts the girls could have gone to school safely enough; in others, no.'

"This I think was a terrible admission." [11]

As the world is to be made safe for democracy, so ought the South to be made free for white women. Is it not the business of the South to endeavor to make the South safe for white women by whatever method appears to be most effective? The women of the South should be just as free to go when, where, and as they please as women in other sections of the country and not be, as has been so aptly put by John Temple Graves, "prisoners to danger and fear":

"In a land of light and liberty, in an age of enlightenment and law, the women of the South are prisoners to danger and fear. While your women may walk from suburb to suburb, and from township to township, without escort and without alarm, there is not a woman of the South, wife or daughter, who would be permitted or who would dare to walk at twilight unguarded through

[11] William Archer, "Through Afro America," London, 1910, p. 22.

the resident streets of a populous town, or to ride the outside highways at midday.

"The terror of the twilight deepens with the darkness, and in the rural regions every farmer leaves his home with apprehension in the morning, and thanks God when he comes from the fields at evening to find all well with the women of his home." [12]

A few words now as to the minor causes of lynching. In reading the annual summary of lynchings given by the *Chicago Tribune,* one may get the impression that Negroes are often lynched for very trifling things. Investigation, however, is apt to show that back of any such lynching was something much more serious than what appears on the face. Many illustrations might be given but one may suffice: thirteen Negroes lynched in Arkansas, March 26, 1904, cause, race prejudice.[13] The following account of this affair is abbreviated from an Arkansas paper: [14]

"Dewitt (Ark.), March 25.—Five Negroes who had been arrested as a result of the race troubles at St. Charles, were taken from the

[12] Address: John Temple Graves, *New York Times,* Sept. 4, 1903.
[13] The Chicago *Daily Tribune,* Dec. 31, 1904.
[14] *Arkansas Gazette* (Little Rock), March 26, 1904. See also *Daily Arkansas Democrat,* March 29, 1904.

guards by a crowd of men last night and shot to death. . . . The five victims make nine Negroes that have been killed within the past week in the vicinity of St. Charles. . . .

"A few days ago a difficulty occurred over a trivial matter at St. Charles between a white man by the name of Searcy and two Negroes by the names of Henry and Walker Griffin. One of the Negroes threatened to knock Searcy in the head with a beer bottle. The trouble was stopped for the time being, but on Monday last the two Negroes met Searcy and his brother in the store of Woolfords and Marsworthy in St. Charles, and the difficulty was renewed. One of the Negroes without warning, struck both of the Searcy boys over the head with a table leg, rendering them unconscious and fracturing their skulls, one of them to such an extent that he may die. The Deputy Sheriff, . . . James Kirkpatrick, attempted to arrest the Negroes and he, too, was knocked down.

"The Negroes then gathered and defied the officers, declaring that 'No white man could arrest them.' Their demonstrations aroused the fear of the citizens of St. Charles and they phoned to this place for a posse to come out and protect the town. P. A. Douglass, deputy sheriff, went out with five men, Wednesday morning. Constable

L. C. Neely went forward with a posse of several men to capture the Griffin Negroes. The constable met three Negroes . . . in the road. He inquired of them if they knew where the Griffins were and one of them replied that they did, but 'would tell no ——— white ———' the Negroes then attempted to draw their pistols, but the posse fired, killing all three of them.

"Yesterday sixteen men left this place for the scene of the trouble. . . . Large crowds in from Roc, Ethel, and Clarenden. During the day while the Sheriff's posse was searching for the Griffin Negroes, they were fired upon by a Negro . . . from ambush. Three of the posse were hit, but the shot used were small, and no serious damage resulted. The posse returned the fire, and a shot . . . felled the Negro to the ground. Several other shots were fired into him, killing him instantly.

"Five other Negroes . . . who were the Negroes that had defied the officers, were arrested, and last night a crowd of men took them away from the guards and shot them to death." The next issue of the same paper stated that two more Negroes had been killed, and the *Daily Arkansas Democrat,* March 29, reported that the Griffins who were the cause of the original trouble had been killed, completing the list of *thirteen.*

The above quotation is given merely as an example of a state of affairs so apt to exist in connection with what usually passes as trivial causes for lynching. May those at a distance from such conditions the better understand!

Thus far I have not discussed lynching in the North, nor do I purpose to do so; but a few words in passing seem pertinent. There is no basis for the assumption, which some seem innocently to hold, that the people of the North are inherently good and law-abiding, while those of the South are inherently wicked and lawless. Indeed, statistics would seem to indicate the opposite.[15] In 1910 over 750 persons to the 100,000 population were committed to prison in New England as against less than 450 in the South. I take it that the people of the North are neither better nor worse than those of the South. The same conditions in either section would produce about the same results. The statistics of lynching I gathered for the North were merely incidental. However, for 1901 and 1902, I find that nine Negroes were lynched in the North, four for murder and five for rape.

Further evidence that the people of the North will engage in lynching when necessity dictates may be had from the early history of California.

[15] Statistical Abstract of the U. S., 1915, p. 55.

Vigilance committees for the protection of the better class of citizens against the disorderly and criminal elements, were organized without warrant of law.   In writing of one of these committees H. H. Bancroft says that it was well represented by men of wealth, intelligence and industry, and that "the largest element comprised men from the Northeastern part of the United States." [16]

. Of remedies for lynching I have none.   Of proposed remedies, I have only to say that those which seem in any way practicable might result in unmerited hardship to whites and an increase in rape cases as well.   Any hope of escape or mitigation of punishment that even unintentionally may be held out to the criminal serves as a wonderful stimulant to crime.   The positive knowledge on the part of those criminally inclined that punishment will be immediate, sure, and adequate, is the best deterrent.   The Negro is a creature that lives in the present and even postponement of punishment robs it of much of its force.   The law sanctions personal self-defense.   The white man in lynching a Negro does it as an indirect act of self-defense against the Negro criminal as a race.

When the abnormally criminal Negro race (partly so, no doubt, because he is not yet ad-

[16] H. H. Bancroft, "Popular Tribunals," Vol. II, pp. 666-7.

justed to his environment) puts himself in harmony with our civilization, if ever, through assimilating our culture and making our ideals its own, then may it be hoped that his crimes will be reduced to normal and lynching will cease, the cause being removed.

CHAPTER IV

THE CRIMINALITY OF THE NEGRO

THE present criminal status of the Negro,—and his criminal record since the Civil War as well,—should cause every member of the race in America to hang his head in shame.

Yet, may it not be that, after all, the Negro is, to a large extent, an irresponsible creature of circumstances, and that his crimes are upon the heads of those who unwisely placed him in a position that he was unable to occupy,—except with injury to all concerned?

Scholars hold that the average citizen of the ancient Athenian Democracy, the greatest of ancient democracies, was as intelligent as the average member of the British Parliament, or of the American Congress. The Negro, however, with all his barbarism and ignorance, totally unrelated to the white man in origin, character, and race, directly after his emancipation, was made a full-fledged citizen in the greatest of modern democracies. The fact is appalling.

Stupidity unsurpassed, unless by the pacifist visionaries of the present day who seek to usher in the millennium by proclamation,—peace treaties, world federations, or leagues to enforce peace. Human nature cannot be changed overnight by edict. When the sun fails to rise wars will cease. It is to be hoped that enough sanity yet remains in the American people to save them from such nonsensical vagaries of sentimental dreamers.

But the Negro, son of a wild and tropical race, content for thousands of years to roam the jungles of Africa, supplied by bountiful nature with all his heart's desire, failing thus to develop any controlling trait of character, or mental stamina, and although civilizations rose and fell beside him, it meant nothing to him. And even now in the midst of American civilization he is moved to action, mainly, by the gusts of primitive emotion and passion. This is the creature that was expected to take an equal share in the government of the most enlightened and progressive people that the world has ever known.

"Who sows to the wind shall reap the whirlwind." So to-day all other domestic problems or questions pale before—"What shall be done about the Negro? The mob acts upon it, conventions of learned sociologists discuss it. Every superficial thinker has a solution of the problem,—ready made, but never in good working order. The Negro is such a problem in our society mainly, no doubt, because he represents the chief criminal element,—how criminal, let statistics, by way of comparison, declare:

In the Northern and Western States in 1910, *one* white person was in a penal institution for every 982 of the white population, and *one* Negro for every 123 of the Negro population; while in the South, the ratio was *one* to every 2014 for the white, and *one* Negro to every 308 of the Negro population. Thus in the North Negroes had eight times their proportion in prison, and in the South six and one-half times. That Negro crime is on the increase is evidenced by the fact that in 1890 the Negroes had hardly six times their proportion in prison in the North, and hardly five times their share in the South.

In this connection statistical tables should be helpful and interesting as well. Table I gives a comparative showing of whites and Negroes in some State penitentiaries. Instead of giving the number of prisoners on hand at a certain time, some prison reports give the number received and discharged during a certain period of time while a few give both. In Table II is given the number of prisoners received by the penitentiaries of a few States during a specified time.

TABLE I

State	Population in 1910		Number in Penitentiary			Times the Number of Negroes to Whites, Year 1910, or Thereabouts
	White	Negro	Year	White	Negro	
Alabama....	1,228,833	908,832	1902	201	525	7 —
			1910	416	1,976	
			1914	357	2,252	
Georgia.....	1,431,802	1,176,987	1905	291	1,989	11
			1910	248	2,300	
			1914	380	2,692	
			1916	412	3,170	
Mississippi...	786,111	1,009,487	1901	107	928	7 +
			1913	156	1,552	
			1915	145	1,336	
Maryland...	1,062,639	232,250	1906	354	586	8 —
			1910	369	663	
			1915	402	682	
Tennessee...	1,711,432	473,088	1910	532	1,236	8 —
			1912	613	1,297	
			1914	651	1,208	
Arkansas....	1,131,026	442,891	1906	244	603	8 —
			1912	213	643	
Texas.......	3,204,848	690,049	1908	1,094	1,987	8 +
			1910	1,119	2,095	
Louisiana....	941,086	713,894	1904	249	1,143	5 +
			1910	382	1,663	
			1915	382	1,663	
Kentucky...	2,027,951	261,656	1911	603	729	9.4
			1915	674	726	
Connecticut..	1,098,897	15,174	1904	419	52	8.4
			1910	542	63	
			1914	578	56	
Kansas......	1,634,352	54,030	1902	874	299	17 —
			1914	508	269	
New Jersey..	2,445,894	89,760	1910	1,049	346	9
			1915	1,020	329	
Ohio........	4,654,897	111,452	1909	1,216	407	15 —
			1911	1,110	417	
Vermont....	354,298	1,621	1904	149	5	12 —
			1910	147	8	17 —
			1912	167	13	
				212	1	

TABLE II[1]

State	Population in 1910		Convicts Received at the Penitentiary During —			Times as Many Negroes as Whites Committed in Proportion to Population of Each Race
	White	Negro	Year	White	Negro	
Arkansas....	1,131,026	442,891	Nov. 1, 1912 to Oct. 31, 1914	606	776	3.4
Alabama....	1,228,832	908,882	Sept. 1, 1910 to Aug. 31, 1914	587	2,414	6 —
N. Dakota...	569,855	617	July 1, 1908 to June 30, 1910	217	11	43
Missouri....	3,124,932	157,452	1906 1909 1910 1912 1914	513 560 543 660 803	306 374 303 389 378	11 +
Maryland...	1,062,639	232,250	Year Ending Nov. 30, 1910	129	199	7 +
Texas.......	3,204,848	690,049	Sept. 1, 1908 to Oct. 31, 1910	835	1,251	
Louisiana....	941,086	913,874	1910 1915	202 257	549 654	4 —
Ohio........	4,654,897	111,452	Year Ending Oct. 31, 1907 Year Ending Oct. 31, 1910	402 504	145 169	14 —
W. Virginia..	1,156,817	64,173	Two Years Ending Sept. 30, 1908	519	428	15

[1] Both Tables I and II have reference to penetentiaries, no account being taken of other penal institutions. The calculations are based upon the census of 1910 and penitentiary reports of the same year, or thereabouts, but some prison statistics for other years are also given.

For the Southern States considered, Table I shows that the number of Negro prisoners around 1910, varied according to the State from five plus times their proportion in Louisiana to eleven times in Georgia. While in the North, the number varied from eight times in Connecticut to seventeen minus times in Kansas. Thus showing that the Negro is everywhere many times more criminal than the white man, and that his criminality is more pronounced in the North than in the South.

That he is discriminated against by the court,—and otherwise,—is sometimes given as a reason[3] for the great criminal showing of the Negro; that for the same kind of crime the Negro gets a much longer sentence than a white man, etc. This is hardly to be held as against the North, and that it is true to any appreciable extent in the South is doubtful, but hard to determine,—absolutely.

As Table I gives the number of prisoners on hand at a certain time and Table II the number committed to prison during a period of time,[2] other things being equal, it is clear that if the Negro is discriminated against through the length of sentence imposed on him by the court, it should be shown by a smaller number being sent to prison

[2] Some State penitentiary reports give the number of prisoners on hand at a certain time, others simply those committed during a period of time, while a few reports give both items.

in proportion to the respective population of the
two races in any State than is to be found on hand
at a certain time.   For instance, at the Maryland
and the Texan penitentiaries, according to the
above tables, in 1910 the numbers of Negroes on
hand were, respectively, eight-minus times and
eight-plus times their proportion, while those committed for the same year were seven-plus and sev-
en, respectively.   This would seem to indicate that
in neither Maryland nor Texas was there but little, if any discrimination against the Negro.   But
a comparison of the statistics for Arkansas and
Louisiana seems to show that the Negro is discriminated against in these States.   However,
upon further investigation it is found that ninety-
one Negroes were sent to the Louisiana penitentiary in 1911 for murder and manslaughter, and
thirty-two for shooting with intent to kill, as
against thirty white men during the same year for
these crimes.   Again, in the Arkansas penitentiary in November, 1912, there were 213 white
and 643 Negro prisoners.   Of the whites but 50
had committed homicide, while 218 of the Negro
prisoners were guilty of the crime.

Moreover, one might naturally expect that the
whites, on account of greater influence, would be
much more likely to secure pardons.   It is doubtful if the whites are thus favored to any large ex-

tent. Between November 1, 1910, and October 31; 1912, Arkansas granted pardons to 121 whites and 86 Negroes, while during the year ending November 30, 1911, Kentucky pardoned nine white men and eighteen Negroes. If statistics were available from all the States it might be rather conclusively demonstrated that the Negro is discriminated against but little by the courts.

In this connection it may be well also to note the fact that in Ohio fourteen-minus times as many as their proportion (according to Table II) were sent to the penitentiary; in West Virginia fifteen times, and in North Dakota forty-three times their proportion.

A comparison of the number of whites and Negroes arrested a year in some of the large cities is given in the following table:

TABLE III

City	Population in 1910		Arrests			White, One Arrest in Every	Negro, One Arrest in Every
	White	Negro	Year	White	Negro		
Atlanta.....	102,861	51,978	1904 1909 1915	6,602 6,241 6,369	10,954 11,925 10,954	16.5	4.5
Baltimore...	473,387	85,098	1905 1909 1915	21,713 20,445 25,108	12,323 11,361 15,840	23+	7.5
Buffalo......	421,809	1,906	1911 1915	23,983 30,711	236 385	18—	8+
Chicago.....	2,139,057	46,226	1907 1909 1915	53,349 62,864 105,119	4,653 4,852 9,508	34+	10—
Charleston, S. C......	27,803	31,069	1907 1911 1913	1,559 1,734 2,487	2,631 2,886 3,185	16+	11—

TABLE III (*Continued*)

City	Population in 1910		Arrests			White, One Arrest in Every	Negro, One Arrest in Every
	White	Negro	Year	White	Negro		
Detroit......	459,926	5,840	1909 1910 1915	10,887 13,726 19,539	775 976 2,121	33.5	6−
Omaha......	119,580	4,516	1907 1910 1915	8,324 9,597 13,091	1,663 2,083 2,211	12.5	2+
Philadelphia.	1,463,371	85,637	1910	71,825	9,507	20+	9+
New Orleans.	249,403	89,672	1903 1910 1913	9,529 15,035 19,486	6,917 10,052 11,163	16.7	9−
St Louis....	645,478	44,541	1904 1910 1913	20,149 29,746 29,166	5,375 8,382 8,099	22−	5+
Providence, R. I.. ...	218,623	5,703	1911 1912	11,332 10,632	434 470	19.3+	13+
Richmond, Va........	80,879	46,749	1904 1907 1910	2,851 4,356 3,710	3,674 5,246 5,893	22−	8−
Wilmington, Del.......	78,309	9,162	1908 1910 1911	3,175 2,933 2,896	963 955 979	26+	9.6
Washington, D. C.....	236,128	94,941	1908 1910 1915	15,985 16,371 17,415	17,430 17,632 17,716	14.3	5.3+

Table III shows that for the cities given, one white person to twenty-one-plus of the white population was arrested during 1910 or thereabouts, but *one* to eight-minus of the Negro. In the cities of the North one to twenty-three whites were arrested and *one* to six Negroes; in the South excluding Wilmington, Del., and Washington, *one* to twenty whites and *one* to eight for the Negroes. In Detroit: *one* for every two plus Negroes were arrested.

In this connection, it would seem that a comparison of the jail population of a Northern and a Southern State might be of interest. For this purpose Alabama and Connecticut were selected. In 1910, Alabama had a white population of 1,228,-832 and 908,282 Negroes while Connecticut had 1,098,897 whites and 15,174 Negroes.[3]

In both Alabama and Connecticut the ratio of whites and Negroes sent to jail during the fiscal year ending September 30, 1914, was about the same, *one* white to four Negroes.[4] However, in Alabama *one* white person to 216 of the white population as against *one* to 54 of the Negro, while in Connecticut, *one* white person to 100, and *one* Negro to 20 was put in jail.

Again, the four counties of Connecticut embracing the large cities of the State, and having nearly all the Negro population, sent to jail *one* white to 92 of the white population, and *one* Negro to 24 of the Negro, or nearly four times their proportion.[5] But in the other four counties with an

[3] My statistics are based on the census of 1910. The Special Report of the Prison Inspector of Alabama for the year ending September 30, 1914, and the returns of the county jails of Connecticut for the same period. As the white population of Connecticut increased about 225,000 during the previous decade, while the Negroes slightly decreased, I added 70,000 to the white population of 1910 to offset the increase of whites during the three or four years between 1910 and 1914. But as both races increased in Alabama I use the 1910 census for that State.

[4] In proportion to their respective population, of course.

[5] In order to avoid repetition, unless otherwise indicated, when

aggregate of 187,058 whites and 1,661 Negroes the ratio was *one* to 174 for the whites, and *one* to 64 for the Negroes or hardly three times as many.

Now, taking the three counties of Alabama in which the cities of Montgomery, Mobile, and Birmingham are located, with an aggregate population of 207,295 whites and 182,211 Negroes, *one* white person to 90 was sent to jail and *one* Negro to 21, or nearly four and one-half times as many.

Moreover, twenty-two counties with no towns of more than 1000 population each, and having a total population of 293,187 whites and 274,533 Negroes *one* white to 523 was sent to jail and *one* Negro to 141, or nearly four Negroes to one white.

Also, in fourteen counties with cities of 1000 to 10,000 population, and a total population of 205,-844 whites, and 207,966 Negroes, the races being almost equal in numbers, *one* white to 400, and *one* Negro to 75 were sent to jail, or six times the Negro's share.

one white to four Negroes or any such ratio is mentioned, the meaning is this: I divide the white population of the state by the white prisoners for the number of white people to each white prisoner, and divide the Negro population of the State for the number of Negroes to each Negro prisoner, and then divide the white prisoners by the Negro to get the ratio of Negro prisoners to the white.

Furthermore, six counties consisting almost wholly of white people, having a total population of 119,496 whites and 5,670 Negroes,—had in jail *one* white to 363 and *one* Negro to 27, or twelve Negroes to *one* white person.

Moreover, eight counties of Alabama, with an aggregate population of 41,323 white and 185,222 Negroes, about four and one-half times as many Negroes as whites, *one* white to 689 were sent to jail and *one* Negro to 156, or about four and one-half times as many.

In studying the jail statistics of Alabama, whether cities or counties, it soon becomes evident that the criminality of the Negro increases as his proportion to the whole population decreases; in other words, the fewer the Negroes in a given population the more criminal they appear. An examination of Tables I, II, and III will show that this is not only true of Alabama, but true, with scarcely an exception, both North and South. Negro crime seemingly increases in the cities and in the North and the West. So does the crime of the white man increase, although not to the same extent.

In general, the denser the population the more likely is friction to occur, or collisions among its units.   But this is not an adequate explanation for the increase of Negro crime.   Nor can it be accounted for except in small part, by attributing it to the more complex social environment of the cities and of the North.   However, it is not to be doubted that the unstable character of the Negro is easily influenced by the temptations incident to city life.   More important, no doubt, is the assumption that where Negroes are few in comparison with the whites, they are more tempted to commit acts of thievery, robbery, and burglary. Again, in the cities, officers of the law are on the watch, consequently more apt to detect and catch a criminal; also, where the Negroes are few they are likely to be held more strictly to the white man's standard of conduct.   However, in some parts of the South, a white man sometimes may be arrested when for the same act a Negro would hardly be bothered.   The idea seems to obtain that for certain things allowance must be made for the ignorance of the Negro, but no excuse is made for the white man.

Again, a great deal of the friction between the two races in the South is caused by the resistance of Negro criminals to officers of the law.   Not only so, but relatives, friends and other Negroes as well often attempt to shield the Negro criminal in order that he may escape detection and arrest. This is not exceptional but rather of frequent occurrence. It is one of the ways in which the black man shows himself to be an enemy of law and order. He does not seem to realize the attitude in which he places his race in acting thus. Now, where the Negroes form a large part or the greater part of the population, it is much easier for him to aid Negro criminals, and it is often effectively done. But where there are but few Negroes in the population, it is to that extent more difficult for the Negro criminal to escape detection and arrest. These seem to be the main reasons why Negroes appear more criminal where there are but few in the population.

In addition to statistics, a few newspaper clippings may aid one more fully to appreciate Negro criminality.[7] It is hardly probable that anywhere in the United States has the Negro, on the whole, had better advantages than in Maryland, Virginia, and Delaware, especially is this true of the Eastern Shore of Maryland. For this reason the following are the more significant:

[7] I made no effort to find these. I give here only a few of those taken from *Baltimore Sun, Baltimore American,* and refer mainly to Maryland, Virginia, and Delaware. What may be true in these States as regards Negro criminality, is likely to be found intensified farther south.

RESISTING OFFICERS, ETC.

"John E. Goode, a Negro, blew off the top of his head at Bedford City this morning in *preference* to *appearing* as a witness against Thomas W. Preston, the Negro murderer of M. D. Custy, a saloon-keeper. . . . Goode was present when the murder was committed. A Negro family named Davis, relatives of Preston, are said to have threatened Goode's life, if he testified." [8]

A Negro in Chestertown, Md., being tried on three charges of arson, attacks the officers of the court:

"Pointing to the Negro, State's Attorney Vickers intimated that he had set fire to the beautiful buildings on the grounds of the Washington College near Chestertown. Suddenly the Negro made a leap for the States Attorney, but was stopped by Deputy Sheriff Brown. The enraged Negro turned and struck the deputy sheriff a stunning blow under the chin. . . . It required seven men to quiet the Negro." [9]

"John Carter, the Negro who shot Policeman Elizabeth Faber and Patrolman George W. Popp

[8] *Baltimore Sun,* Jan. 6, 1910.
[9] *Baltimore News,* Oct. 20, 1916.

on October 17 on the Edmondson Avenue bridge when they attempted to arrest him died in the city jail at 3.10 o'clock yesterday morning." [10]

"The final decision in the Brownsville incident is closed finally and the verdict will give entire satisfaction to everybody except Hon. Joseph Foraker of Ohio; the Negro soldiers who shot up the Texas town and their *comrades who concealed the guilt of the bloodthirsty marauders.*" [11]

"Negro soldiers of the Twenty-fourth United States Infantry had planned a riot of bloodshed among the white residents of Houston (Texas) August 23, two days before the deadly attack which cost the lives of 15 Houston citizens last month, according to the report of the Civilian board of inquiry which reported to the Houston City Council to-night. . . .

"The committee says that the undisputed and convincing testimony of witnesses proves that the Negro soldiers went forth to slay the white population indiscriminately: that no Negro was hurt or molested by them, not one Negro house was fired into, and that the Negroes were warned beforehand . . . to stay off the streets." [12]

[10] *Baltimore Sun,* Aug. 4, 1915.
[11] *Ibid.,* April 8, 1910.
[12] *Ibid.,* Sept. 12, 1917.

"The police of the Northwestern district are looking for about 25 Negroes who late Saturday night attempted to break down the front door of the boarding house conducted by Miss Mary Ashten at 906 McCulloh street." [13]

"Centerville, Md., Jan. 7.   The Rev. J. D. Jackson, colored, pastor of Bethel-African Methodist Episcopal Church, was arrested and placed in jail here to-day charged with housebreaking and burglary." [14]

"Middletown, Del.—The Rev. Aaron Gibbs, a Negro preacher, is being held in $500 bail for court for alleged theft of 280 pounds of meat from the farm of Daniel Ford, near this place. The meat was recovered at the home of Gibbs by Chief of Police, Lee Cochran." . . .

"Another Negro, Arthur Brewington, wanted for theft of meat and chickens held the whole Smyrna police force at bay for hours, until his ammunition gave out.   He then retreated escaping from the force into a deep swamp five miles away." [15]

[13] *Baltimore American,* Feb. 18, 1913.
[14] *Baltimore Sun,* Jan. 8, 1917.
[15] *Ibid.,* Feb. 21, 1917.

"Seaford, Del., July 3.—Negroes who live in and around Bridgeville attempted to take the town last night. . . . About 10 o'clock at night the Negroes began firing among themselves, and Bridgeville being without police protection, was at the mercy of their revolvers, which were being fired in rapid succession. The town seemed to be alive with brawling blacks, and several fights were started in different parts of the town. At the railroad station a large crowd collected and fired shots in every direction. At a colored church another crowd got together, firing desperately among themselves. The citizens being utterly helpless stayed in their houses behind locked doors." [16]

NEGROES AT PICNICS AND ON EXCURSIONS

"Federalsburg, Md., Aug. 14. John Henry Lake, a Hurlock Negro, was killed and Frank Dickerson wounded, perhaps fatally, at a celebration by Negroes last night." [17]

"Gettysburg, Pa., Sept. 11.—Clara Brown, of Baltimore, colored, was shot in a brawl here in the course of an excursion and picnic. Her condition is critical. Three other persons were also injured. The picnickers had a gay frolic. It is

[16] *Baltimore Weekly Herald,* July 8, 1909.
[17] *Baltimore Sun,* Aug. 15, 1914.

charged that fifty of them attacked a policeman, and one of them robbed Robert King of Hunterstown of $35. There were about 7240 excursionists. Gettysburg has made a protest." [18]

"Roanoke, Va., March 29.—Drunken Negroes took charge of an excursion train between this city and Winston-Salem last night and as a consequence Sidney Wood of Winston-Salem is dead at Martinsville, and two-score other Negroes are more or less wounded. Knives, razors, and pistols played prominent parts in the melee. . . . The train was stopped several times by Negroes pulling the bell cord, and the train was cut in two several times, leaving a number of coaches behind with a second section following. . . . The three coaches which were cut off were filled with white people. . . . When the train reached Bassetts, in Henry County, every Negro in two coaches was apparently in a fight. The screams of the terror-stricken women added to the excitement." [19]

NEGROES AT CAMP MEETING

"Smyrna, Del., Aug. 9.—As has been the case yearly for a dozen years there was a fatal shooting affray at the Negro camp meeting at Friend-

[18] *Cambridge* (Md.) *Record,* Sept. 12, 1913.
[19] *Baltimore Sun,* March 30, 1910.

ship last night.   Howard Hollis, a Negro of Clayton, Del., was shot in both legs during the fight. . . . It is not known who shot Hollis as bullets were flying thick and fast during the melee." [20]

"Federalsburg, Md., Sept. 6.—Officers are scouring lower Caroline County to-day for four Negroes who last night shot up a Negro camp-meeting at Mount Hope, near this town." [21]

"Deputy Sheriff Bruce C. Dean, yesterday afternoon shot and killed a Negro named Smith at what is known as Henry's Cross Roads [near Cambridge, Md., negro] campmeeting. . . . There has always been more or less disorder; in fact, it is generally known that fights, cutting affrays, and a general disregard for the law exists." [22]   The Negro who was killed shot at the deputy Sheriff when he tried to arrest him.

"Salisbury, Md., Aug. 23.—A riot occurred last night at the Negro campmeeting, on the west side of the county, and Asbury Waters, 19 years old, was killed, and Clinton Gosless was shot through his jaw-bone and his chin carried away by a bullet.

[20] *Baltimore Sun*, Aug. 10, 1915.
[21] *Ibid.*, Sept. 7, 1915.
[22] *Cambridge* (Md.) *Record*, Aug. 25, 1913.

"Just at the height of the services one of the local preachers, was raising his hands in prayer, a colored woman slipped into the kneeling crowd and pulled a pistol from her dress folds and fired a bullet into his heart. Waters pitched forward and died instantly. . . . Immediately after, Sallie Milburn whipped a pistol from her pocket and blazed away at Clinton Gosless, the bullet entering his jaw. Gosless is in a very serious condition with little hope of his recovery."

Both these accounts were in the same issue of the *Cambridge* (Md.) *Record,* but the camps were in adjoining counties.

Indeed, Negro camp meetings and bush meetings had become so numerous,—occupied such a large part of the Negroes' time during summer, caused so much lawlessness among them; and consequently so much expense to the whites, that the Maryland Legislature in 1916 passed a law evidently directed against them, which in part is as follows:

"It shall be unlawful for any person, persons, association or organization of any kind whatever to hold any camp meeting or bush meeting within the limits of Talbot, Caroline, Dorchester, Somerset, Kent, and Worcester Counties without first making application in writing at least fifteen days prior to the date of such camp meeting or bush meeting therein.   That such application for a permit as aforesaid, shall be accompanied by a petition in writing signed by at least twenty-five tax payers, each of whom shall reside within three miles of the place where such camp meeting is to be held, and each petition shall have annexed thereto as a part thereof an affidavit to the effect that each of the said petitioners are bona fide tax payers and of their residences within three miles of said place of such proposed meeting.   And whenever the County Commissioners of any of the respective counties shall have any reasonable grounds that any lawlessness or disorder will occur, at said camp meeting or bush meeting, they shall refuse to grant such permit, and if, after issuing any permit to hold any camp meeting or bush meeting there shall be lawlessness or disorder reported to said County Commissioners, it shall be the duty of said officials to investigate or have investigated by the Sheriff or other officer of said county, the matter, and upon proof of said lawlessness or disorder they shall forthwith revoke said permit and it shall be the duty of the Sheriff, or other officer of the respective Counties to enforce the provisions of this act."

In about the same spirit and for the same purpose, the reduction of Negro crime, a few years ago, the city of Mobile, Alabama, passed an ordinance, an account of which is taken from a Baltimore periodical: [23]

"The police department of Mobile, Ala., has established a curfew law for Negroes. Commencing on the night of July 21, the law provides that all Negroes must be in bed at their homes by ten o'clock or be subject to arrest. Any caught wandering at large after that hour will be locked up. This action is taken because there is said to be an epidemic of hold-ups perpetrated by the Negroes. If such a law was enforced in Baltimore it would decrease the alley fights ninety-five per cent."

NEGRO IMMORALITY

In connection with Negro criminality it seems pertinent to say something of Negro immorality. Two of the Negro's most prominent characteristics are the utter lack of chastity and complete ignorance of veracity.

The Negro's sexual laxity, considered so immoral or even criminal in the white man's civilization, may have been all but a virtue in the

[23] *Methodist Protestant,* July 28, 1909.

habitat of his origin. There nature developed in him intense sexual passions to offset his high death rate. Then, too, the economic influences which fostered a family life among other peoples were mostly lacking in tropical Africa as nature provided abundantly without effort on the part of man.

Although the regulations adopted by masters for the control of the Negroes during slavery times may have served as a check upon their natural sexual propensities, however, since emancipation they have been under no such restraint and as a consequence they have possibly almost reverted to what must have been their primitive promiscuity. Huffman says that in 1894 more than one-fourth of the colored births in the city of Washington were illegitimate. Many prominent Negroes admit that above ninety per cent of both sexes are unchaste. A negro may be a pillar in the church and at the same time the father of a dozen illegitimate children by as many mothers.

Another Negro failing is lying. One can believe neither layman nor minister, neither criminal nor saint among them. One may occasionally find a truthful Negro,—just as he may find a virtuous or an honest one. Undoubtedly both honest and truthful was the Negro,—an elder in the church,— who refused to partake of the Lord's Supper, because, as he said, the flour the bread was made of had been stolen.

Some benevolently-inclined men and many religious zealots thought that religion and education was the "Open Sesame" by means of which the "salvation" of the Negro was to come. So they sent him money to build churches and to found great schools. Many, however, are now finding that though the Negro may have religion he has no morality; and that too often his education makes him unwilling to do what he can do and wish to do that for which he is unfitted or for which there is no demand. At present who can tell whether he is going forward or backward. Some one has said that there is going on side by side in the Negro people a minimum of progress with a maximum of regress.

However, the Negro takes great pride in his church, and in his way is intensely religious. The late Booker T. Washington said:

"Of these millions of black people there is only a very small percentage that does not have formal or informal connection with some church."

It is, indeed, likely that more than one-half of the male Negro adults are actual members of church, while not more than *one* in four or five white male adults have such connection.   Notwith-standing such a showing, religion does not seem to have any controlling influence over the life and character of the Negro.

Nevertheless, the Negro enjoys his religion, for he is an emotional animal.   It is the emotional element in religion that appeals to him and makes his face to shine.   The promise of never-ending pleasure in a world to come may be but faintly comprehended by him, but the fear of a far off punishment deters him but little from crime. He is the optimist of the human race, and lives in the eternal present.   He has no sorrows from the past, and no care except for the immediate future. He keeps without effort or intention two injunctions of Scripture: "Visit the sick," and "have no care for to-morrow."

He goes to camp meetings or revivals, sings, prays, and shouts until the small hours of the night.   He may think he thus pays the Lord His due, even though the next day, if he works at all, he sleeps on the plow-handle, or with half-closed eyes cuts up the tobacco or the cotton.

However, he may be free from the painful necessity to work the next day, if his wife or mother should have just returned from a white neighbor with an "apronful," even if he did not visit some tempting smoke-house or hen-roost on the way home from his religious revelry.

How can Negro criminality and immorality be lessened? The answer is not easy, and what follows is merely suggestive. Up to the present, what little the Negro has accomplished, in most part has been due to the white blood he has received, or to white direction and sympathy. The Negro is woefully lacking in initiative and persistence. He would be greatly benefited by some sort of probationary oversight. If the Filipinos are not fit for self-government collectively, much less the Negro individually. A great part of them are no more fit to profit by their freedom than so many children. Nothing so promotes health of body and strength of character as regular and persistent industry. To the Negro should be preached the "gospel of salvation" through work. Somehow get him to work six days in the week, instead of working two and loafing four, as many now do. Industrial schools such as Hampton and Tuskegee meet a great need but they touch but few.   "

If the States had the power to train or even to enforce habits of industry and thrift upon the shiftless, idle, and vicious Negroes it would undoubtedly result in measureless benefit to both white and black. Liberty should not be made

a "fetish." If the Negro has rights that should \
not be abridged, so have the white people rights
and *lives* that should not be endangered. The
law-abiding many have the right to protection
from the criminal few—actual or incipient. With
the adoption of some such scheme the Negro might
gradually cease to be a menace to the white race.

Again, so often the Negro leaders of the Negro
race are merely blind leaders of the blind,—entirely lacking in breadth of view, often discour-
aging in their race what they should encourage
and encouraging what they should discourage as
the following quotation may indicate:

" 'Make lynching a Federal crime, and stop
turning the murderers over to local authorities
who are in sympathy with them,' demanded Dr.
W. T. Vernon, of Memphis, Tenn., before 15,-
000 Negroes, who were celebrating the twenty-
fifth quadrennial Conference of the African M. E.
Church in Convention Hall, Broad street and Al-
legheny Avenue, yesterday." [24]

Such talk as this serves to promote Negro
crime. If instead of Negro leaders writing ar-
ticles for magazines and Negro papers, in ser-
mons in Negro churches, and in addresses before

[24] *Philadelphia Record*, May 8, 1916.

Negro conventions denouncing the whites for protecting themselves against Negro crime in their own way, could realize that it is not so much the black skin as what sort of man the black skin covers, that counts, would demonstrate to their black brothers that they themselves are the sinners rather than the sinned against, that they are the transgressors rather than otherwise, they might accomplish much toward lessening Negro crime. If such leaders would use their influence to the utmost to make their race as law-abiding as the whites, and should bring it about, it is hardly likely that then they would need to complain that their race is imposed upon. But if they were, at least, there would be more force in their complaint. But so long as the Negro race commits its present amount of crime, the complaint against unfair treatment is more than childish.

CHAPTER V

SEGREGATION OF THE NEGRO

IT is hardly to be questioned that since the Civil War the white man and the Negro have been drawing farther and farther apart. Religious teachers, political adventurers, and fortune hunters gave the first great impetus to the movement. The teachers, however, misguided, may have been sincere in their efforts to benefit the Negro; but the carpet-baggers had in mind only personal aggrandizement.

This political separation of the Negroes from the Southern whites was the entering wedge that split asunder the ties that had bound the two races together. Otherwise the Negroes might have divided with the whites between two or more political parties. This would have resulted greatly to their advantage for each party would have bid for their vote.

Upon the passing of the carpet-bag administrations, however, the Negroes lost most of their political importance. Since then it has been further reduced until it is now almost a negligible quantity.

During the Reconstruction period, the attitude of the Negroes served to alienate their former masters, who undoubtedly would have otherwise been their best friends. Between most of the Negroes and the poor whites of the South, there had always existed a feeling of mutual dislike if not contempt. After the War great numbers of the latter secured wealth and influence. Their dislike of the Negro, however, has increased rather than abated.

Thus, the Negroes began to feel the lack of that sympathy, consideration, and direction from the whites to which they had been accustomed. Therefore, whether consciously or unconsciously, they turned to leaders of their own color more readily, and this has gradually developed a feeling of race solidarity. However, this should not be an unmixed evil.

Again, in many parts of the South, the industrial development of the past thirty years has furthered segregation in that section by drawing the whites to the towns and cities. But Negroes have also turned to the cities in great numbers notwithstanding the fact that the industrial enterprises of the cities usually hold out but little if any inducements to such migration. This has given rise to the agitation for the segregation of the races in the cities whether voluntary or by legal enactment. While this is more pronounced in the South it has also spread to the North and West.

One of the most noteworthy examples of voluntary segregation is to be found in New York City:

"In one district of New York City a Negro population equal in numbers to the inhabitants of Dallas, Texas, or Springfield, Mass., lives, works, and pursues its ideals almost as a separate entity from the great surrounding metropolis. Here the Negro merchants ply their trade; Negro professional men follow their various vocations; their children are educated; the poor, sick, and the orphan of their race is cared for; churches, newspapers, and books flourish heedless of those outside this Negro community who resent its presence in a white city." [1]

Indeed, in many parts of the country the Negroes have separated themselves from the whites by founding small communities of their own. In almost any state, villages and towns populated and governed almost exclusively by Negroes may be found. A few of the more important are: Buxton, Iowa, 1000 whites and 4000 Negroes;

[1] *The Outlook,* Dec. 23, 1914.

Brooklyn, Illinois, 1600 Negroes; Balor, Oklahoma, 3000; Plateau, Alabama, 1500; Mound Bayou, Mississippi, 700.[2]

In addition, there are almost an unlimited number of what may be termed Negro settlements scattered over the country. Such is Petersburg, on a railroad two miles from Hurlock, Maryland, which may serve as an example. It consists of about twenty-five houses and lots or little farms, altogether embracing about one hundred acres. These are mostly owned by the Negroes who live on them. They bought these little tracts several years ago when the land was considered almost worthless as it was so sandy and poor. The men till their lots and occasionally work by the day for some of the surrounding white farmers. In season, the women and children and some of the men as well go elsewhere to pick berries. In the late summer all have employment at home for about two months furnished by a white cannery, near. Altogether it seems to be a very contented community. Each Negro is his own boss and can work when it suits him and stop when he pleases. To make such a living as satisfies him he need work scarcely half of his time. This just suits Negro inclinations and consequently Petersburg is a little paradise for the Negro.

[2] "Negro Year Book," 1914-1915.

However, the segregation of the Negro is not yet universal. In some towns and cities as well both North and South they are more or less scattered. In the City of Washington they are found practically everywhere. In most cities they occupy the most undesirable parts—such as any low muddy places or narrow alleys. In some small cities of the South, while there may be a well defined Negro section, nearly every well-to-do family has a Negro servant family in the back yard. La Grange, Georgia, is an example.

But in the greater number of towns and cities the Negro section and the white section have been clearly defined for years. Cambridge, Maryland, —a city of about 5000 whites and 2000 Negroes,—is of that sort. All the Negroes live in the Southwest section except two or three families that live in a kind of alley near the bridge which connects East Cambridge with the main part of the city. One sees but few Negroes on any white street, not even on the main business street except Saturdays when they do their shopping. But on the street just west of the main business street and parallel with it, the business street of the Negro section, only a few whites are ever to be seen but it is always black with Negroes. Here are Negro grocery stores, a drug store, barber shops, theater, schools, and churches. Very few mulattoes are in evidence for the Negroes are nearly all of pure blood. One never hears of any serious trouble between the Negroes and whites of Cambridge for they live in comparative harmony with one another. At East New Market in the same county, a railroad separates the white from the Negro section of the town, while at Vienna, eleven miles distant, the Negro section is several hundred yards from the white part of the town.

Although Negroes constitute about one-third of the population of the Eastern Shore of Maryland, they have not become sufficiently numerous as farmers as to cause much injury to farm land or to farming interests, whether by careless and indifferent farming or by making the country districts undesirable to white people as places of residence. Most of the Negroes in the country districts are used by the white farmers as farm hands. Negroes are seldom able to rent the better grade farms while those owned by them are usually small and poor. As a consequence most of the land on the Eastern Shore is in a high state of cultivation and the farmers prosperous and contented.

In most parts of the farther South, however, except Texas and Oklahoma, and the Piedmont and mountain sections, the whites have allowed the

Negroes to gain such a foothold in the country districts that they are now the greatest obstacles to agricultural progress. The South is just beginning to realize the true condition of things.

Indeed, already in North Carolina an agitation has begun for the segregation of the Negro in the rural districts. If this could be accomplished in all parts of the South it would be a wonderful boon to that section. Not only would it to a great extent free the white women from fear of attack by Negroes but this would serve to attract to the South thrifty and ambitious farmers from other parts of the country. A more satisfactory social life could be developed in the rural districts. Adequate schools and churches could better be maintained, not only for the white race but for the Negroes as well. As a consequence both races would be benefited.

With the exception of the establishment in the South of separate schools for the whites and the Negroes, only in comparatively recent years has segregation been brought about by law. More than twenty years ago, however, a few Southern States had laws providing for segregation in railroad travel and now almost every Southern State has such a law. In some, Maryland for example, the law also applies to passenger steamboats. A certain section of the boat is given to the Negroes.

Both races have now become so accustomed to these laws that they are generally taken as a matter of course.

Lately many Southern cities have passed ordinances extending the principle of segregation in travel, to street cars. Mobile, Alabama, however, as early as 1902 had such an ordinance in force. As it was one of the first, and but slightly different from those in force in other cities, the main part is quoted here, as follows:

"All persons or corporations, operating street railroads in the city of Mobile or within its police jurisdiction shall provide seats for the white people and Negroes when there are white people and Negroes on the same car by requiring the conductor or other employe in charge of the car or cars to assign to passengers to seats in all the cars, or when the car is divided into two compartments in each compartment, in such manner as to separate the white people from the Negroes, by seating the white people in the front seats and the Negroes in the rear as they enter the car, but in the event such order of seating might cause inconvenience to those who are already properly seated, the conductor or other employee, in charge of the car, may use his discretion in seating passengers, but in such manner that no white person and Negro must be placed, or seated, in the same section, or compartment arranged for two passengers: Provided, That Negro nurses having in charge white children, or sick or infirm white persons, may be assigned to seats among the white people." [3]

The conductor is also given the authority of police officer to enforce the law.

The form of segregation which is receiving most attention in the South at present, however, is the effort of various cities,—great and small,—to provide by law, for (as nearly as possible) distinct residential sections for the two races. This question was first agitated in Baltimore 'in 1809. A segregation law was passed but it was soon pronounced invalid by the courts. In 1911, another such ordinance was put in force but it, too, was declared void, first by the Criminal Court of Baltimore, and later by the Maryland Court of Appeals. The latter Court, however, maintained that the city has the right to pass a segregation law. I quote the following words of the court:

"This Court is of the opinion that the Mayor and City Council of Baltimore may, in the exercise of its police power, validly pass an ordinance for the segregation of the white and colored races

[3] Code of Mobile, 1907, p. 330.

without conflicting with the Constitution of the United States or of the State of Maryland." [4]

Very soon after this, another ordinance was passed. It has now been in operation about four years (1917). However, the Maryland Court of Appeals is holding a case *sub curia*, awaiting a decision of the United States Supreme Court in a case testing the validity of the segregation law of Louisville.[4a]

In 1912 the Virginia Legislature enacted a law for the purpose, it seems, of encouraging the cities and towns of that State to segregate the whites and the Negroes. Richmond, however, had already passed a segregation ordinance in 1911. It is as follows:

"That it shall be unlawful for any white person to occupy as a residence or to establish and maintain as a place of public assembly, any house upon any street or alley between two adjacent streets in which a greater number of houses are occupied as residences by colored people than are occupied as residences by white people.

"That it shall be unlawful for any colored person to occupy as a residence or to establish and maintain as a place of public assembly any house

[4] *Baltimore Sun,* Aug. 6, 1913.
[4a] Found void by U. S. Supreme Court, Nov. 5, 1917.

upon any street or alley between two adjacent streets on which a greater number of houses are occupied as residences by white people than are occupied as residences by colored people.

"That no person shall construct or locate on any block or square on which there is at that time no residence any house or other building intended to be used as a residence without declaring in his application for a permit to build whether the house or building so to be constructed is designed to be occupied by white or colored people, and the Building Inspector of the city of Richmond shall not issue any permit in such case unless the applicant complies with the provisions of this section.

"That nothing in this ordinance shall affect the location of residences made previous to the approval of this ordinance, and nothing herein shall be so construed as to prevent the occupation of residences by white or colored servants or employes on the square or block on which they are so employed.

"Every person, either by himself or through his agent, violating, or any agent for another violating any one or more of the provisions of this ordinance shall be liable to a fine of not less than $100 nor more than $200, recoverable before the police justice of the city of Richmond, and, in the discretion of the police justice, such person may, in addition thereto, be confined in the city jail not less than 30 nor more than 90 days." [5]

Some of the principal reasons for the demand for the segregation of the two races in towns and cities are given in the *Preamble* to the Virginia law of 1912 as follows:

"Whereas the preservation of the public morals, public health, and public order, in the cities and towns of this Commonwealth is endangered by the residence of white and colored people in close proximity to one another: therefore, be it enacted by the General Assembly of Virginia," etc.

The effect upon public order of the "close proximity" of the two races may best be shown by the following quotations:

"Having occasion to ride on the Guilford Avenue car last week, going down town, there were 10 or 12 Negro men in their dirty working clothes. On one seat there were two of them; the other 8 or 10 had each of them a separate bench. Refined handsomely dressed women entering the car had to stand or sit beside one of these dirty Negroes.

[5] *Baltimore Sun,* Aug. 8, 1913.

I am not an enemy to the race. I believe they should have as good accommodations as we have, but they should be to themselves." [6]

"I prefer rubbing elbows with them (Negro guano factory laborers) to riding with the so-called respectable Negroes on the Preston Street and other cross-town lines. On the Preston street line in particular conditions have become so unbearable that the writer, who formerly used this line to reach his place of business, has been obliged to adopt a more circuitous route, which takes fully twice as long.

"On this line respectable white people and white women especially, are subjected to every species of affront and insult, which they cannot resent without risk of being drawn into a dispute, in which no decent person cares to be involved. The Negroes realize this and it emboldens them still further." [7]

"Residents in the 1300 block, Myrtle Avenue were greatly excited yesterday by a colored family moving into 1334 during the morning. The block is occupied by white people and this is the first intrusion by Negroes." [8]

[6] Letter to *Baltimore Sun*, March 11, 1914.
[7] *Ibid.*, Aug. 18, 1913.
[8] *Baltimore Sun*, Aug. 22, 1913.

"Angered because a colored family had moved into house No. 128 Patapsco Avenue, a crowd of about 100 residents of Pimplico gathered before the dwelling last night and battered it with sticks and stones until every window pane was smashed, valuable chandeliers demolished and plaster knocked in great clouds from the walls." [9]

"About 150 determined white men gathered early yesterday evening at a house on Mattfeld Avenue, near Falls road, and camped on the grounds until a Negro family of two men and three women and two children living in the house left. . . . After the Negroes had found a place the men scattered. . . . No violence or cruelty was meant toward the Negro family, but that the neighborhood was determined to show that it was white and meant to stay white." [10]

Indeed, objections are often made to the location of Negro churches, schools or Y. M. C. A.'s in or near white neighborhoods. The following newspaper headings may be sufficient to indicate the situation:

"Relay [Md.] Objects to Negro College," [11] "Mount Washington Up in Arms Over the Plan

[9] *Baltimore American,* Sept. 21, 1911.
[10] *Baltimore Sun,* May 19, 1916.
[11] *Ibid.,* January 13, 1914.

to Locate Morgan College [Negro] There," [12] "Lafayette Square Protests Against Putting a Colored School On Its Borders." [13]

Nor is this attitude toward the Negro confined to the South. If the North had as many Negroes in proportion to its population as the South, the feeling there would be just as acute. The following quotations so indicate:

"Boston, March 23.—Refusing to associate with Dr. Melissa Thompson, a Negress of North Carolina, who has been appointed a physician in the maternity department of the New England Hospital for Women and Children in Roxbury, five young white women doctors sent in their resignation." [14]

"Boston, Sept. 8.—Here where years ago a mob of exclusive Back Bay residents stormed the old courthouse to free a Negro from his Southern master, descendants of the Back Bay rescuers to-day are fighting against serving as election supervisors with a Negro, whose appointment became known Wednesday." [15]

[12] *Baltimore Sun,* August 26, 1913.
[13] *Ibid.,* Aug. 14, 1915.
[14] *Ibid.,* March 24, 1911.
[15] *Baltimore American,* Sept. 9, 1911.

"Ithaca, N. Y., March 28.—The petition of more than 200 women in Cornell University against the admission of [Negro] women into the only dormitory in the University has been forwarded to President Schurman." [16]

"New York, July 2.—Twenty teachers, about half the staff at Public School No. 125, in Wooster Street, Manhattan—have applied for transfers, owing to the assignment by the Board of Education of William L. Burkley (mulatto) as head of the school." [17]

"Burlington, Vermont, dislikes the idea of having the Tenth Cavalry at Fort Ethan Allen. The Tenth happens to be a colored regiment and the prospect of having 1200 Negro soldiers within three miles of the city is greatly exciting many of the people of Burlington." [18]

"Akron, Ohio, August 13.—A serious race riot may take place if notices posted on the homes of North Side Negroes last night by members of a citizens' 'Vigilance league' in that section of the city, who have warned the Negroes that unless

[16] *Washington Times,* March, 28, 1911.
[17] *Baltimore Sun,* July 3, 1909.
[18] *Democrat and News,* Cambridge, Md., Sept. 3, 1909.

they sell their property and leave that section of the city, they will be forcibly evicted from their homes, which are also threatened with destruction.

"Members of the 'Vigilance league' declare today that the Negroes are practicing a form of blackmail by buying property in the fashionable residence district of North Hill, which they occupy until their white neighbors pay an exorbitant price for their property to get rid of them.

"They say several instances of this kind have been recorded recently and feeling against the Negroes reached a high pitch at a secret meeting held last night. The public have taken every precaution to guard against a serious outbreak.

"The Negroes have been given one week in which to sell their property and leave that section of the city by the 'Vigilance league.' " [19]

"Bellville, Ill., Oct. 7.—Ten of the 13 Negroes who have been on trial here for a week, charged with the murder of Detective Samuel Coppedge on the morning of July 2, which precipitated the East St. Louis, Ill., race riots were convicted today and sentenced to 14 years in the penitentiary. Three were acquitted." [20]

[19] *Baltimore American*, Aug. 14, 1913.
[20] The *Philadelphia Record*, Oct. 8, 1917.

"York, Pa., Aug. 20.—Dr. George W. Bowles, a Negro physician, has started a movement here for the segregation of his race. Bowles believes that Negroes would be better taken care of if in one part of the town. Now the blacks are housed in the alleys and few are permitted to rent houses on the main streets." [21]

A few such Negro leaders as Dr. Bowles, just mentioned, seem to appreciate the advantages of segregation for the Negro, and for both races. Others, however, object to segregation because to their minds, it is a denial of social equality with the white race, or that they are deprived of the best living conditions. If the Negro had the proper race pride he would welcome the opportunity to live among his own race. He would delight in the companionship of those of his kind. Among the Negroes would develop grades of society as among white people. Indeed, already in Baltimore Druid Hill Avenue and other streets have become a sort of aristocratic section for the Negroes. Those who have money have the opportunity to live among their own race in the best manner possible.

Other races are so proud of their traditional grandeur or present attainments as to claim su-

[21] *Baltimore Sun,* Aug. 21, 1913.

periority and exclusiveness. But the Negro has such little race pride that were it possible every Negro man would have a white wife and every Negro woman a white husband. Many Negro leaders are so lacking in race esteem as to seize every opportunity to force themselves into the society of other races. And although they possess a strong sense of their rights they are usually found unmindful of attendant obligations.

The great mass of Negroes, however, soon accommodate themselves to segregation regulations, whether for schools, railways, or for the residential sections of cities and seem to care but little about the question of equality. It is only when stirred up by the unwise of their own race, or by some sentimental, if well-meaning, but shallow-thinking whites, who have lived far removed from association with Negroes, that they manifest much interest in such matters.

In association among races, unless there is some strong cementing influence to counteract it, friction is likely to occur between them in proportion to racial difference. And so long as racial antipathy shall exist—and practical minded men see no signs of an end of it in the near future—regulations for the promotion of harmony should be encouraged by both whites and blacks.

It would be almost as reasonable to expect an

idiot and a genius to find a common ground of association as to expect it of a white man and a Negro. For in both races there is a failure to recognize that consciousness of kind which is the basis of all pleasant association. Indeed, even the subdivisions of the white race show a strong preference each for those of his own division. An Italian prefers to associate with an Italian; a German, with Germans; and a Jew, with Jews.

So, in the last analysis, the most potent reason for the segregation of the whites and the Negroes is their unlikeness. For they are antipodal in the extreme: the nadir and zenith of peoples. This dissimilarity cannot be removed by soap and water, time, charity, education, or culture. After all these it will yet remain.

Another reason for segregation is the criminality and immorality of the Negro race. Even if it would benefit a few Negroes or satisfy their vanity to travel with whites or to live on the same street with them is little reason why the comfort, property values, health and morals of the whites should be endangered thereby. The better elements of society have rights as well as the worst and the majority should receive consideration as well as the minority. It is in strict accord with sound ethical principles that laws should aim to level up rather than to level down.

Again, the susceptibility of the Negro to dis- \
ease is another very potent reason for segregation laws. The Negro's manner of living since
his emancipation—irregular in every way, sometimes half-starved—together with their immoral
habits, have so weakened the constitutions of a
great part of them that they easily become victims
to disease.

According to the *Washington Post* (March 3,
1917) of 20,000 Negroes who had lately arrived
in Philadelphia from the South 1000 were ill with
pneumonia and tuberculosis, of whom 700 were
said to be dying.

The "Negro Year Book" for 1914-15 makes
the statement that 450,000 Negroes in the South
are seriously ill all the time, and that 600,000 of
the present Negro population will die of tuberculosis. When one recalls that thirty-five years
ago tuberculosis among Negroes was scarcely
heard of, he may the better appreciate the full
force of the above statement in regard to tuberculosis among Negroes.

In a letter calling a conference in Baltimore to
consider better housing conditions for the Negro,
Mayor Preston said:

"The insanitary housing of many of our colored people and the congestion within the area in

which they reside are developing breeding for disease. The condition is a serious menace to the general health of the city. It threatens to become in the future a matter of such gravity as to challenge the thoughtful consideration of our entire community. . . .

"The high death rate in Baltimore is occasioned by the high mortality among the colored people. The death rate from tuberculosis alone is three and a half colored to one white." [22]

The Health Department, in a bulletin issued about the same time, showed that the death-rate per thousand of the Negro population of Baltimore was 33.96, while that of the white population was but 16.91. What is true of Baltimore is more or less true elsewhere.

It is needless to consider other reasons for segregation laws, the three given; viz., to lessen friction, to check criminality and immorality, and to prevent the spread of disease, are sufficient warrant for segregation laws of whatever kind.

[22] *Baltimore Sun,* Feb. 20, 1917.

CHAPTER VI

NEGRO WEALTH OR POVERTY,—WHICH?

THE statement sometimes made that in 1865 the Negro was a landless and penniless race is far from the truth. Some slaves had property that they had secured through opportunities given them by their owners. No doubt free Negroes secured at least a small share of the public domain. Many slaves upon being given freedom by benevolent masters, were also given money or property at the same time.

Cases of this sort were frequent during slavery times. Several such instances are given in the *Staunton* (Va.) *Democrat* during 1846-1848. Such cases as the following were not uncommon:

"A Negro man named Lerr; age about 35 years; a slave for life $700." "A negro man named Jacob; age about 24; a slave from life—$600." [1]

[1] *Baltimore Sun*, Dec. 18, 1909.

These were two items in an inventory of the estate Phillip B. Saddler returned to the Orphans' Court of Baltimore in 1860.

Even *The Liberator* mentions some cases of the kind. For example:

A man in Kentucky *willed* to his slaves, whom he made free, horses, wagons, farming implements, and $4,000. Another, also in Kentucky, freed a Negro family of four, purchased an excellent farm for them, paying fifty dollars an acre, and in addition gave them a wagon, a pair of mules and a quantity of provisions. These are given merely as examples of what was constantly taking place.[2]

Indeed, there were many rich free Negroes in the South at the time of the Civil War. Although there is abundant evidence that the free Negroes, as a rule, were an indolent, thriftless, and even vicious class, some of them, no doubt on account of the reënforcement of white blood in their veins, were industrious and prosperous.

At Charleston, S. C., alone in 1860, there were 355 free Negroes who paid taxes.[3] Of these 226 owned real estate valued at $1,000 or more, each.

[2] *Liberator*, Jan. 20, 1854, and Nov. 9, 1860.
[3] *Ibid.*, May 11, 1860; E. Collins, "Memories of the Southern States," p. 44.

Some of them had $10,000 to $40,000 worth of property. Altogether they had almost $1,000,000 worth.

In Louisiana also, as might be expected, there were many wealthy free Negroes. Most of these were descended from the French and the Spanish planters and their Negro slaves. One free Negro family of Louisiana was said to be the richest Negro family in the United States before the War, having property valued at several hundred thousand dollars.[4] Frederick Law Olmsted, who traveled through the State about 1855, was told that some of the free Negroes owned property worth $400,000 or $500,000, which included some of the best sugar and cotton plantations. Indeed, all over the country might have been found free Negroes with more or less property. The greater part of it, no doubt, had been given them by white masters or white relatives.

In reference to the amount of property held by Negroes at the time of the Civil War, William H. Thomas, a Negro writer, says:

"We have no trustworthy data by which to measure the wealth of those residing in the North, though it is known to have been considerable;

---

[4] *Liberator,* March 18, 1859. Also, Olmsted, "Seaboard Slave States," pp. 633-640.

but in the South, where separate racial statistics were kept, the value of property owned by free Negroes was between $35,000,000 and $40,000,-000."

In 1860, there were in the neighborhood of 250,000 free Negroes in the South and around 225,000 in the North. Then, if the free Negroes of the South had nearly $40,000,000 it would seem a fair estimate that in both sections the free Negroes had at least $60,000,000. Taking this for granted, as money at six per cent compounded, annually, doubles every twelve and one-half years, the $60,000,000 at interest until the present (1917) would have amounted to about $960,-000,000. If the 10,000,000 Negroes of the country at present had as large amount of property in proportion, as the less than 500,000 free Negroes of 1860, they would be worth more than $1,200,-000,000.

However, in 1903, it was estimated by a committee of the American Economic Association that all the taxable property in the United States owned by Negroes in 1900 amounted to only $300,-000,000. The $60,000,000 at six per cent would have amounted to about $400,000,000 by that time.

In 1913, in an address before the Negro Business League which met in Philadelphia, Booker T. Washington said that Negroes pay taxes on $700,000,000 worth of property. Many other students of the Negro question both black and white have placed about the same estimate upon Negro holdings. Even if true, the amount would be about $200,000,000 less than the $60,000,000 at interest to the same time.

Now, assuming that Negroes actually owned $700,000,000 worth of property in 1913, what does it signify? The value of all property in the United States is now estimated at almost $250,000,000,000. Now, suppose that it was $210,000,000,000 in 1913, this would be just three hundred times the estimated value of Negro property at the time. In other words, 10,000,000 negroes owned one three-hundredth as much as 90,000,000 whites. Thus one white man on an average would have as much as thirty-two Negroes.

Even were it true that the Negro race began with nothing after the War, likely thousands of white men who became millionaires had just such a start. One such white man, especially, is, no doubt, worth as much as the 10,000,000 Negroes claim to be, even though he has given to charity almost half as much more.

Indeed, the $700,000,000 in question is but little more than two-thirds as much as the whites in the United States, according to the *Chicago Tribune*,[5] gave to charity during 1916. Again, the $700,000,000 lacks nearly $200,000,000 of being equal to the taxable basis of Baltimore. It would be difficult to secure statistics in reference to the matter, but there could be little doubt that the first immigrants to the United States after the Civil War, including the descendents of such to the number of 10,000,000,—immigrants who came with practically nothing, no money in the majority of instances and ignorant,—now are worth many times $700,000,000.

The $700,000,000 may also be considered from another point of view: The "Negro Year Book," 1913 credits the Negro with $700,000,000 worth of property and speaks glowingly about the increase of the previous ten years. The statement is made that farm land and buildings owned by the Negro increased from $69,639,426 in 1900 to $273,506,665 in 1910, and that during the same period the total value of Negro farm property, including live stock, and implements and machinery increased from $177,408,688 to $492,-898,216.

Now, the Census shows that in 1900 Negroes

[5] The *Chicago Tribune*, Dec. 30, 1916, gives a list of gifts to charity during 1916 as near $1,000,000,000.

owned 13,770,801 acres of land entire and 2,205,-297 acres in part. If their share of the land owned in part were half, then, the Negroes had in possession 14,873,449 acres. In 1910, they owned 15,961,506 acres entire and 3,114,957 acres in part. Allowing them the same share of that held in part as for 1900, gives them in 1910, 17,518,-984 acres. However, only about two-fifths of the land owned by Negroes is arable, the larger part being woodland, swamp, rough and stony land, much of which is almost valueless.

According to the "Negro Year Book," Negro farm land and buildings increased in value from $7.98 an acre in 1900 to $17.40 an acre in 1910.[6] If this is true; the value of the Negro lands and buildings in 1900 was $118,690,124 instead of $69,639,426; and in 1910, $304,830,032 instead of $273,506,665.

[6] According to the census, "The average value of farm property per acre was $27.01 for farms operated by Negroes in 1910 as compared with $13.08 for 1900, and $47.72 for farms operated by whites in 1910." There was no indication whether all land or merely arable land is meant. About three-fourths of the farms operated by Negroes are rented. Observation convinces me that farms owned by Negroes are not more than half so valuable an acre on the average as the land rented by them, for from necessity they buy the least valuable land. This being true, Negro lands in 1900 could not have been worth more than $6.00 an acre and about $13.00 in 1910. However, in making any calculations as to the value of Negro lands and property, I will take the Negro Year Book estimate and apply it to all Negro land.

Again, Negroes operated in 1910, 893,370 farms while but 241,221 of these were owned or partly owned by them. An idea of the value of the farm stock on these farms, and the Negroes' lack of thrift as well, may be had from a statement made before the Negro Conference at Tuskegee Institute in 1915:

"An investigation has shown that there are 20,000 farms of Negroes on which there are no cattle of any kind; 27,000 on which there are no hogs; 200,000 on which no poultry is raised; 140,000 on which no corn is grown; on 750,000 farms of Negroes no oats are grown; on 550,000 farms no sweet potatoes are grown, and on 200,-000 farms of Negroes there are no gardens of any sort."[7]

According to the Census, however, on farms operated by Negroes, farm implements and machinery increased from $18,859,757 in 1900 to $34,178,052 by 1910, while live stock increased in value from $84,936,215 to $184,896,771. Adding to these amounts for 1910 the above sum of $304,830,032 for Negro lands and buildings a total of $523,904,855 is obtained for 1910 instead of $492,898,216, which is the *Negro Year*

[7] Scott and Stowe, "*Booker T. Washington*," p. 171.

Book estimate.[8]   So here credit may be given the Negro for the larger amount.

Again, according to the Census of 1910, Negroes owned around 220,000 homes other than farm homes.   No estimate as to their value is given.   Although $400 each is undoubtedly a high valuation they may be roughly estimated at that.   This amounts to $88,000,000.   Booker T. Washington claimed for Negroes just before his death, 43,000 business interests.[9]   The observation of the writer is that Negro business interests average much less than $1000 each.   Indeed, great numbers not more than $100 or $200 each.   However, if they average $1000 each they amount to $43,-000,000.

By adding the three items: $523,904,855, the

[8] The estimate of $7.98 an acre in 1900, and $17.40 an acre in 1910, according to the "Negro Year *Book*" mentioned above, is undoubtedly too high by at least one-third, but I use it so as to give them the advantage rather than otherwise.   I know a body of 1,300 acres of land in my own county, Dorchester, Md., consisting of some cleared land, woodland and brushland, which a real estate man told me could be bought at five dollars an acre. This is such land as the Negro usually buys.   Only a short distance from the body of land mentioned in this note land is valued at from twenty-five to one hundred dollars an acre.

[9] Among the Negro business interests are 64 banks which are often mentioned in Negro speeches.   It seems, however, that two of them have failed.   The total capital of these banks is said to be $1,500,000.   In striking contrast are the 27,000 white banks with $2,162,900,000 capital.   Petersburg, Negro settlement in Md., mentioned above, has two Negro stores with hardly $100 worth of goods, each.

value of Negro farm property; $88,000,000, Negro-owned homes other than farm homes; and $43,000,000, the value of the Negro business interests; a grand total of $654,904,855 is obtained. Thus it would appear that in 1913 Negroes might have had around $700,000,000 worth of property in their possession.

Naturally the next question that comes to mind is this: How much does the Negro owe?

Scarcely without exception the white man is his creditor, consequently what the Negro owes is to be subtracted from the amount of his possessions.

According to the Census of 1910, something like 65,000 Negro farms and 50,000 Negro-owned homes have mortgages or similar encumbrances against them. It is unlikely that this is true to any large extent except as regards the more valuable Negro properties. If the average farm mortgage is $500 and the average home mortgage $300 both together will amount to $47,500,000. It is reasonable to suppose also that the 43,000 business interests owe at least $15,000,000.

Again, while more than 150,000 Negro farms and about as many more Negro homes were reported by the census as free of encumbrance, nevertheless, it is not unlikely that they owe a large amount of money in notes, bills, etc. Nor need it be forgotten that often Negro tenants owe their landlords fully as much as the entire value of such tenant's personal property.[10]   Many Negroes in one way or another owe about as much as they are worth.   This is undoubtedly true of some white men, also, but the point is, what Negroes owe they owe to white men.   A well-to-do farmer told the writer a few years ago that he held various kinds of small claims to the amount of more than $4000 against the Negroes of his community. So, $50,000,000 should not be an excessive estimate for such Negro liabilities.

By adding these various items; $47,500,000 in mortgages and liens against Negro farms and homes; $15,000,000 against Negro business interests; and $50,000,000 against Negro farm owners, home owners, tenants, etc., gives a grand total of $112,500,000.   Subtracting this from $654,904,855, which was found to be the value of Negro property, leaves $542,404,855 as the value of Negro property when debts are paid.

Again, in regard to the statement above that Negro farm property increased in value from $222,485,096 in 1900 to $523,904,855 in 1910 one may need to be reminded that live stock and land about doubled in money value during this

[10] I make no mention of the little personal property often not taxed many poorer Negroes possess, for the reason that usually such Negroes owe retail store keepers even more than their little property would sell for.

time and that by 1913 they had more than doubled. This was due mainly to the wonderful increase in the output of gold mines thus making money cheaper. With this depreciation in the value of money the Negro, of course, had nothing to do.

Except for this, it is unlikely that the $222,-485,096 the valuation of Negro farm property in 1900 would have increased to more than $265,-000,000 in 1910 instead of $523,904,855. For during the time the Negro added but 2,645,535 acres which may be valued at $21,000,000. The remaining $23,000,000 being sufficient to allow for the improvement of the land, if any, and any actual increase of cattle and farm machinery. Now, subtracting $265,000,000 from $523,904,855 leaves $258,904,855 which was due to rise in price rather than to effort on the part of the Negro. Again, subtracting the $258,904,855 from $542,-404,855, the value of all Negro property after their debts were paid, leaves $283,500,000 which, except for the circumstances over which the Negro had no influence, would have been the actual wealth of the Negro about 1913, instead of $700,-000,000 as claimed.

Of this amount, no doubt, quite a large part was given to individual Negroes by whites for one reason or another. I have already adverted to the fact that during slavery times Negroes often received both money and property from kind-hearted masters, along with their freedom. How much has been given them since emancipation would be hard to determine. Only a short while ago, indeed, the *New York Tribune* mentioned a white woman who had left her Negro maid $12,-000 in cash, and other valuables in addition.[11]

Moreover, it has been estimated, that of the $28,496,946, the value of plant equipment and endowment of Negro private schools, five-sixths was contributed by whites and only one-sixth by Negroes.[12] During the years 1912 and 1913 white people gave nearly $2,000,000 towards Negro education.[13] Nor does there appear to be any falling off in the white man's gifts to Negro schools. In the early part of the year 1917, the Rockefeller Foundation appropriated to American schools and colleges $575,200, of which $197,000, several times their share, was given to Negro schools.[14] In addition, Federal and State institutions for the higher education of the Negro have an income about $1,000,000 and property valued at $6,000,-000.[15] Nor is this all, no doubt, Southern whites

[11] *New York Tribune,* Jan. 25, 1917.
[12] "Negro Education," Government Printing Office, 1917, Vol. I, p. 8.
[13] U. S. Educational Report, 1914, Vol. I, pp. 612-13.
[14] *Baltimore Sun,* Jan. 30, 1917.
[15] "Negro Education," Government Printing Office, 1917, Vol. I, p. 12.

have contributed several times as much to Negro education by taxation as has been given otherwise.

Again, the amount of money and lands that the Negro secured during the reconstruction period might be an interesting subject for investigation. The Negro legislator had the same privilege as the white one to sell his vote and influence. Nor could there be little doubt that he failed to use the opportunity. The following story is credited to Senator Z. B. Vance of North Carolina: [16]

A Negro member of the North Carolina legislature was found chuckling to himself over a pile of money which he was counting. "What amuses you so?" he was asked. "Well, boss," he replied, grinning from ear to ear, "I's been sold in my life 'leven times, an' fo' de Lord, dis is de fust time I eber got de money."

During the Reconstruction period taxes became so oppressive that thousands and thousands of farms and plantations were sold at auction for taxes. In some places land became almost valueless. It is hardly to be doubted that many Negroes who got easy money through politics at this time failed to use some of it in the purchase of land.

[16] James Ford Rhodes, "History of United States," Vol. VI, p. 305.

Now, what is the reason for the poverty of the Negro? Indeed, from the foregoing it must appear that poverty is a more appropriate word to use in such connection than wealth. The answer is not far to seek. It is the natural result of the Negro character, disposition, and training. The following letter is suggestive :

" . . . 'I have done my work practically the whole summer with the exception of a few weeks that I had a trifling no account Negro, and even then I had to do the best portion of it in order to get them to accomplish anything. When they would wash and iron, those days I did everything else and they helped a little with the ironing, for if I didn't they would never get through. They [Negroes] are absolutely worthless, and if I didn't have small children I wouldn't let one light within a mile of me. . . . " [17]

A Negro who worked in the strawberry section of Delaware told the writer a few years ago that although he usually worked in the daytime he roved about every night. It happened that once, when he had been carousing as usual on the night before, that he was put to harrowing strawber-

[17] Quotation from a letter shown to the writer, which was written by a woman in Richmond.

ries. About three o'clock in the afternoon the overseer came along and found that he was harrowing up the strawberries from one end of the row to the other,—he was so sleepy. The overseer simply told him to put his horse in the stable and go to bed, which he did. As he got some sleep, when night came he was out again for a great part of the night; and so on.

As a laborer, the Negro is not so satisfactory as formerly. The old-time Negro, trained in slavery to work, has about passed away and his successor is far less efficient and faithful to duty. Lately, large numbers of Negro laborers have shown a tendency to leave the farms for work on railroads, in sawmills, and in the cities, large numbers migrating to the cities of the North. They like to work in crowds and this often results in making more work for the police.

From the good wages Negro laborers have received for several years, many of the more farsighted have saved enough to buy little homes. A few of the more ambitious may continue to save, but far the greater part are then perfectly satisfied and settle down to a life of ease and contentment. By raising a hog or two, a few chickens, some garden vegetables, and, with a day's work now and then, they pass their time in a way suited to their indifferent nature.

A concrete example may be of interest. A pure Negro, about thirty-five years of age, a few years ago, purchased about half an acre of land on the bank of a "branch" near a small village in Maryland. For a few dollars he bought an old discarded house about one hundred and fifty yards away, and with the aid of neighbors moved it on his lot. It is doubtful if both the lot, and the house (after being moved and repaired) cost him more than one hundred dollars.

This Negro has been living in it for years and seems perfectly contented. His family consists of himself, wife and three daughters eleven to seventeen years of age. The surrounding country is one of the best tomato growing sections in the United States and during about six weeks of the tomato season tomato pickers are in great demand and make good wages. During this time the Negro man and his family usually work hard; for they pick by the basket and make in the neighborhood of two hundred dollars. This is practically their year's work. The remainder of the year they do but little. They have a garden, pigs, and chickens. It would be an easy matter for this family to get ahead in the world; but they prefer the easy life of comparative idleness,—for this was their incentive to secure a home.

This is also one of the main reasons, no doubt,

for the great increase in Negro tenant farmers, especially that of share tenants. The latter class increased about thirty-six per cent between 1900 and 1910. Many of these seldom work a full day at a time. As they usually put off cultivating a crop to the last moment, if a wet season happens to set in, it is soon greatly damaged by a growth of grass. As a tenant farmer, the Negro realizes that he is more independent, his time is his own, and that he can usually work when he pleases. A great part of his time is given to various Negro recreations,—such as visiting, riding and driving, crap-shooting, preaching, attending revivals, and camp-meetings.

So the cause of the Negro's failure to secure a reasonable share of wealth is not lack of opportunity,—for (at least, in the South) he has every opportunity that he could wish in order to do so,—but rather to his racial traits or characteristics,—some of which are: a happy-go-lucky disposition, indolence, shiftlessness, laziness, indifference, lack of mental stamina and ambition, and strong criminal tendencies.

CHAPTER VII

THE FUTURE OF THE NEGRO

MANY solutions of the Negro problem have been proposed. Men so gifted with imagination that they do not find it necessary to consider either logic or facts, over and again, in a single speech or magazine article, have solved it to their individual satisfaction. Such proposed solutions are usually no less preposterous than visionary. With these I have nothing to do. As elsewhere in this study, so also here, I consider only what seems to have a firm basis of fact.

However, in passing, I may be pardoned, if I have the temerity to suggest the following, which, although seemingly fanciful, yet may have sufficient ground in reason as to merit some consideration: If about 100,000 square miles of territory on the Gulf of Mexico, embracing, say, Louisiana east of the Mississippi River, excepting New Orleans,—the southern part of Mississippi and Alabama, the part of Florida south of Alabama, and a small part of southwest Georgia, were set apart as a State or States to which all the Negroes in other parts of the country be encouraged or obliged to migrate, it might result in great good to both races.

Something like half the population of this section are Negroes, while the whites that are here are mostly in the towns and cities. The area suggested is more than that of New York and Pennsylvania combined. There would be room for all Negroes in the country for generations to come. As the Negro states would be members of the Union, with representatives and senators in Congress, the Negroes would have an opportunity under the Federal Government to develop a political and social world of their own removed from the overshadowing presence of the white man. If the Negro showed himself unable to develop the power of local self-government under such an arrangement, his case would be absolutely hopeless. However, there are so many difficulties in the way and so many objections that might be made that no one need either hope or fear that any such thing will ever be undertaken.

But somewhat more in keeping with common sense and prevalent ideas is the proposal that Negroes be encouraged to distribute themselves equally over the country; thus relieving the South of its burden of Negro population. If such an equalization of the Negro population could be carried out, the Negro then being everywhere few in numbers to the whites, could the better be held to the white man's standard of conduct. Not only so, but the Negro would have an opportunity to absorb the white man's civilization more quickly, if ever. In addition, the race question would cease to be sectional, and laws mutually advantageous to both races could then be passed.

Before going further, even at the risk of digressing,—for it is a matter of justice to the Negro,—it should be said in favor of the Negro that even though he is the most alien race among us, no question as to his patriotism is ever raised. He has fought in all our great wars and has shown himself patriotic to the core.

A day or two after President Wilson had made his German War address before Congress, the writer happened by the *Star* bulletin board in Washington, and noticed a German talking to a big burly Negro against war with Germany. He pointed to the bulletin board and told him not to believe anything he saw there for it was all lies made in London. The Negro seemed to listen in a half-disgusted sort of way, but as he started off he was understood to say:

"I wish I was with some colored soldiers in Europe. We would show the Germans how to fight."

The Negro has no kindred country to look to, so he is undivided in his allegiance. This cannot be said of all other races among us,—not of the Japanese and Chinese who seek admission at our Pacific shores. Like the Negro they cannot be assimilated by our people. In numbers, however, they would constitute a much more dangerous element to our welfare and safety than the Negro. Japan is almost abreast of our civilization and the western nations are doing their best to train China to be an antagonist worthy of their steel, should she ever have cause to cross swords with them. Large numbers of Chinese and Japanese would not only add to our race problems but would increase our chances for friction with their home governments. In addition they might constitute a reverse army of the enemy in our midst in case of war. But no such danger need be feared from the presence of the Negro.

I have just adverted to the fact that the yellow race and the black are not easily assimilated with the white race. It may be well that it is so. To the normal white man amalgamation with these races is almost unthinkable. Nevertheless, there are a few misguided individuals who surely have either a mental or a moral twist who persist in joining together that which nature has put asunder.

A few years ago, a minister sent the following telegram to the Governor of California:[1]

"I have just married a Japanese to an American and have done more for God and Uncle Sam than the alien land bill will do in 1000 years."

It is not the ungodly that cause the suffering in the world so much as the bigoted if well-intentioned fools. Self-elected good people can usually be counted on to cause a lot of mischief. If those who set themselves up as leaders and ethical teachers would but first make sure that they were possessed of at least a fair amount of common sense!

In a recent Methodist Conference at Roanoke, Virginia, the statement was made that the records of some churches in Massachusetts show that in the previous year "17 per cent of the marriages were those in which Negro men married white women or white men married Negro women."[2] This is the more remarkable when account is taken of the very small Negro population of that State.

It is even sometimes asserted that the Negro would bring to the white race some qualities which would tend toward the development of a more perfect man. But such an idea has no basis in fact. The following quotation is to the point

[1] *Baltimore American*, May 23, 1913.
[2] *Baltimore Sun*, March 30, 1917.

"We have ample experience to go upon in South America, in the West Indies, in the Southern States themselves. The mulatto exists and has existed for generations, not in hundreds or thousands, but in millions; in what respect has he proved himself the superior of the pure Spaniard, or Portuguese, or Anglo-Saxon? Does South American history bear testimony to his political competence? Have his achievements in science, in literature, in music, been superior to the un-Africanized peoples? Or waiving the question of superiority, has he ever in these domains, produced meritorious work in any fair proportion to his numbers? I do not say that it is impossible to make out a sort of case for him, by the ransacking of records and the employment of a very indefinite standard of values. But I do most emphatically say that no conspicuous or undeniable advantage has resulted from the blending of bloods, such as can or ought to counteract the instinctive repugnance of the South." [3]

It is said that an investigation of 2200 Negro authors showed that nearly all of them come from the mixed stock.[4] How many of these would take

[3] William Archer, in *McClure's,* July, 1909.
[4] C. A. Ellwood, "Sociology and Modern Social Problems," p. 241.

first, second, or even third rank in the literary world? It is needless to answer. Indeed, Negroes and mulattoes have been toilers in the United States for generations but who ever heard of an important labor saving instrument invented by them? The same abilities or characteristics which would make a white man only locally important would make a Negro or a mulatto famous. There were thousands upon thousands of white men intellectually and otherwise superior to Booker T. Washington who gained but little recognition, but because he was a negro, or rather mulatto, Washington's abilities stood out in striking relief. Mulattoes ought to furnish the leaders of the Negro race for the best white blood runs in the veins of some of them. Although mulattoes may furnish the Negro leaders, there can be no doubt that they also furnish far beyond their share of the vicious and the criminal elements of the race as well.

It may be pertinent in this connection, however, to observe that in the South the two races have been gradually drawing apart, amalgamation or miscegenation is becoming more and more repugnant, the conditions which favored it do not obtain to anything like the extent as formerly, as a consequence the mixing between the whites and the blacks is rapidly lessening. Although the census shows an increase in the number of mulattoes from decade to decade, the increase is mainly due to the mixing of mulattoes with pure Negroes.

Some students of the subject, who seemingly are more familiar with the conditions in the North and the border States than with those of the farther South, sometimes estimate from one-third to one-half of the Negroes in the United States to be mulattoes. This, I am confident, is a mistake. I was reared in a border State, have spent some time in the North as well as in several Southern States, and have been in many of the leading cities of the South. My observation leads me to believe that the Census, in this respect, is more nearly correct than any other source of information.

The Agents of the Census, in 1910, were instructed to "report as 'black' all persons who were evidently full blood Negroes and as 'mulattoes' all other persons having some proportion or perceptible trace of Negro blood." Accordingly in a population of 9,928,000 Negroes in the United States there were found to be 2,050,000 mulattoes, 20.9 per cent, or a little more than one-fifth.

By geographic divisions the percentage of mulattoes among the Negroes was as follows: New England, 33.4 per cent; Middle Atlantic States, 19.6; East North Central, 33.2; West North Central, 28.7; South Atlantic, 20.8; East South Central, 19.1; West South Central, 20.1; Mountain, 28.6; and Pacific States, 34.7.

Of the Northern States, Michigan took first place, with 47 per cent of mulattoes among her Negroes. Maine was next, with 45.9; and Wisconsin third, with 39.4. Those with the smallest percentage were Wyoming, 13.1 per cent; New Jersey, 15.8; and Pennsylvania, 19.2. The Southern States having the largest percentage were, Virginia, 33.2 per cent; West Virginia, 32.5; and Missouri, 28.4 per cent. A large number of States in the South had a small percentage of mulattoes among their Negroes: Maryland, 18.6 per cent; Georgia, 17.3; Mississippi, 16.9; Alabama, 16.7; South Carolina, 16.1; Florida, 16.0; Delaware, 11.9; and the Eastern Shore of Maryland which borders Delaware on two sides, had only 11.1 per cent, or *one* mulatto to every nine Negroes; thus the Eastern Shore has the distinction of having fewer mulattoes in proportion to its Negro population than any other section. It is therefore evident that in the North the proportion of mulattoes among the Negroes is from about one-fifth to almost one-half; while in the South the proportion ranges from above one-eighth to about one-third. In the States where the bulk of the Negro population is found it is only about one-sixth. With slight exceptions, it seems to be true that the fewer to the white population the more mulattoes there are in proportion to the number of the Negroes.

Indeed, may it not be true that the much larger proportional number of mulattoes among the Negroes of the North in no small measure accounts for the greater proportional amount of crime among the Negroes of the North? So it would appear that the amalgamation or miscegenation of the whites and the Negroes is not a leveling up but rather a leveling down process; at best nothing otherwise than building up the Negro by lowering the white. So no greater nor more fearful calamity could befall the white race in America than that the Negro should lose his identity through being absorbed by this great division of the Anglo-Saxon race.

Again, many optimistic white men have thought that the Negro could be raised to the white man's level by means of the training and culture that comes through the study of books. To these education for the Negro has been a watchword. To a large extent Southern whites have been in sympathy with the education of the Negro. Indeed, many years ago, contrary to what one not familiar with the South might suppose, a prominent man in North Carolina in seeking a congressional nomination on a platform hostile to Negro education failed even to carry his home county. And efforts to restrict the amount appropriated to Negro schools to the part of the school taxes paid by Negroes have failed.

Since 1870 the South has spent on Negro education around $230,000,000 and is now appropriating for that purpose near $10,000,000, annually. It is doubtful if the Negro contributes in taxes even half the amount spent on his public schools. In 1912, according to the Educational Report of that State, North Carolina spent $436,-480.08 for Negro teachers and Negro school buildings, of which the Negro contributed in taxes for schools $190,378.81, or a little more than two-fifths. Texas spends not far from $2,000,000 a year on Negro schools, and Georgia about $850,-000. The District of Columbia, indeed, spends more per capita on Negro pupils than on whites. However, this is a notable exception.

There are also more than six hundred private and denominational schools of secondary and college grade in the United States for the higher education of the Negro. The property of these is valued at about $28,500,000.[5] From 1865 to 1917 about $65,000,000 has been contributed to Negro education in the South through various religious and philanthropic organizations.

[5] Negro Education (Government Report), Vol. I, p. 8.

But notwithstanding the fact that the illiteracy of the Negro race had been reduced by 1910 to about thirty-three per cent, there is a widespread feeling of disappointment in Negro education. Not that it has made the Negro more criminal as has sometimes been said, however, this is not yet well determined, but rather that it has failed to make him a greater producer, or to aid him to adjust himself to economic conditions. Instead of firing him with the desire to do more and better work, too often he quits it altogether.

As a teacher or a preacher the Negro has a wide field for his race needs him and the State and the Church pay him. But as a doctor, lawyer, or other professional, poverty and pauperism (the condition of the greater part of the Negro race) militate against them. In addition, the Negro has not yet sufficient confidence in the professional skill of those of his own race as to cause him to employ them exclusively.

There is a growing conviction in the South that the first aim of Negro education should be to fit the Negro for the opportunities of his social and industrial environment. Also that it should endeavor to strengthen his will power, in order that he may overcome his constitutional inertia; and that it should give him a knowledge of sanitary living, thus preventing disease.

In the South Carolina Public School Report for 1915, the State Superintendent of Schools has this to say:

"The Negro is here and is here to stay. He cannot remain ignorant without injury to himself, his white neighbors and to the Commonwealth. His training should fit him for the work that is open to him. . . . While industrial education is needed for both races it is especially desirable for the Negro.

"The money now expended for Negro education is largely wasted. Can we afford longer to allow this large element in our population to follow their present practices and remain in their present condition?"

Such schools as Hampton Institute and Tuskegee have fairly well demonstrated that industrial education is at least a good thing for the Negro. In these and other such schools thousands have been given an inspiration for a higher plane of living. Indeed, it is claimed that very seldom is any graduate of these two schools convicted of crime:[6] The influence of Tuskegee on the Negro in a material way may be appreciated by the statement that in 1881 when the school was opened in

[6] "Education and Crime," *South Atlantic Monthly*, January, 1917.

Macon County, Alabama, not more than fifty or sixty Negroes in the county owned land, but in 1910, 503 Negroes in the county owned 61,689 acres, "probably the largest amount of land owned by the Negroes of any county in the United States." [7]

If a few Negro industrial schools make such a good showing, then why not multiply the number? Indeed, it is yet too early for either the Negro or his friends to indulge in too much optimism in regard to the matter. For while it may be true in general that whatever is done in behalf of a lower element in a society benefits the whole society, at the same time, it needs to be borne in mind that to the extent that it is done to the cost or by the neglect of a more homogeneous and wholesome element in the society or if it in any way militates against such element it is a questionable proceeding.

What if the industrial education of the Negro should be found to conflict with the interests of the white laborer or skilled worker? Does any one suppose that it is the purpose of the South so to educate the Negro (or even allow him to be so educated) as to enable him to take the bread from the white man's mouth? And does any one suppose that the laboring white man of the arrogant

[7] Scott and Stowe, "Life of Booker T. Washington," p. 176.

and aggressive Anglo-Saxon race will stand tamely by with folded arms while there is danger of its being done?

This is the central point of the whole situation. But in the South the contest between these two conflicting interests is not yet, as the demand for labor skilled or unskilled is too great. The Negro has had and can have all the work he wants and more for the asking; indeed, often his labor is anxiously solicited. How long this will continue no one knows, positively. However, when the population of the country reaches 150,000,000 or 200,000,000 then labor will likely be as plentiful here as it is now in Europe. Then, the labor of the Negro will hardly be solicited, rather otherwise. The white man's sympathetic attitude toward the Negroes' many shortcomings is fast passing. When the Negro is required to measure up to the white man's standard and is found wanting, what remains for him?

Furthermore, the Negro might as well get fully in mind that, although the white man sometimes may win without merit (yet often fails to win even though deserving to do so), for the Negro himself, even though merit may not win, without it he will have absolutely no show. He must be not only as well adapted to an occupation, or qualified for it, as a white man but better.

Until lately those especially interested in the welfare of the Negro might have entertained the hope that he would hold his place in his customary occupations or even make them in great part his very own. This would have been a kind of segregation to occupation analogous to his segregation as regards residence and at least as advantageous to him. But in hardly more than one occupation is such the case. As a porter he seems to have the field practically to himself, and as hod-carrier he is in demand. But as a barber he has fast been losing ground. The Negro as a waiter takes more pride in his occupation and is more polite and obliging than the white man of the waiter class but he is even being displaced in this work. Even as a farm laborer, for which service he has been trained for generations, he is losing his grip. "Too slow, unreliable, inefficient" are some of the counts against him.

The idea that prevails outside the South that Negroes do practically all the work on Southern farms is far from the truth. More than half of the cotton crop is raised by white labor,—in Texas, three-fourths or more. Even in sugar and rice fields white labor is getting common.[8] Often, indeed, a farmer will not employ a Negro if he can get a white man.

[8] Year *Book*, Dept. of Agriculture, 1910, p. 193.

Indeed, the Negro farm laborer and the Negro farmer are the greatest stumbling-blocks in the way of the agricultural development of the South. Were it possible to remove from the South at least three-fourths of these and replace them with whites whether native or foreign there can be no doubt that the production of Southern farms would be wonderfully increased. It is an injury to the South and to society as a whole that the Negro has under his control even as much land as at present. When his "slipshod" farming gives place to more scientific and businesslike methods there will be more farm products for distribution.

The inefficiency of the Negro as a farmer is strikingly shown by a study of the conditions in several Mississippi counties:

"Lowdnes County with three Negroes to one white man, having 21,972 blacks and 7121 whites, requires 3.15 acres to make a bale of cotton, while James County, with three whites to one negro, having 13,156 whites and 4,670 blacks, requires 1.98 acres to make a bale. The farm lands of Jones county are valued in the census reports at $2.85 per acre and the farm lands of Lowdnes County at $9.83 an acre. Yet the poor lands of Jones County under intelligent cultivation produced nearly twice as much per acre as the rich lands of Lowdnes County when cultivated mostly by Negroes . . . in every comparison made between a white county and a black one the black was the most fertile, yet the white was nearly twice as productive." [9]

Such a poor showing for the Negro almost persuades one that he deserves to be supplanted by whites in farm work and in farming, even if he should not be. At present the South holds out unequaled attractions in the way of climate, rich soil, and cheap lands, to those of other sections of the country who may be seeking farm homes. And there can be little doubt that with the passing of the free public lands the tide of immigration in the near future will set in that direction, in spite of the presence of the Negro. Then what will become of the Negro when he shall have to compete with the thrifty hard-working Poles, Bohemians, and native Americans from the North and the West? Will he be simply pushed aside and left to gravitate to a still lower level? Nothing will save him unless he soon wonderfully changes in habits and disposition. So the Negro may as well look forward to the time when he will be sup-

[9] Quoted by A. H. Stone in "American Race Problem," pp. 177-8, from J. C. Hardy, "The South's Supremacy in Cotton Growing," p. 9.

planted in these occupations to which he thinks himself so well adapted and in which he thinks himself so well fort:fied,—those of farm laborer and farmer.

Finally, may not the unquestioned physical deterioration of the Negro since his emancipation as shown by his susceptibility to disease together with his high death rate portend the ultimate practical extinction of the race in the United States? During slavery times the Negro was fairly well fed and usually worked according to set regulations. Evidently such food and training had no little to do with developing a sound body, and disciplined his mind to some extent as well.[10]

According to De Bow, the mortality of the free Negroes before the War was a hundred per cent greater than that of the slaves. It even appears that the death of the Negroes in the South at that time was less than that of the whites. In Charleston, S. C., the average death-rate from 1822 to 1861 was 25.98 a thousand for whites and 24.05

[10] "There were imported in the British West Indies 4,000,000 Negro slaves and when they were manumitted there were 800,000. Into the Southern States 400,000 were imported and there were before the war 4,000,000; this decrease in the former and increase in the latter are strong facts. The climate influence was on the side of the West Indies. There must have been a very different treatment."—Charleston (S. C.) *Mercury,* Nov. 23, 1863. Quoted by it from a London paper, written by an Englishwoman who had spent a short time in the South.

for Negroes. About the same was true of some other cities. From 1865 to 1894, however, the average death-rate at Charleston was 26.77 a thousand for whites and 43.29 for Negroes.[11] No doubt the slight increase of the death rate among the whites was due to the rapid increase among the Negroes as the whites necessarily came more or less in contact with the Negroes.

Indeed, very significant in this connection, is the statement made in the "Negro Year Book" (1914-15) that an average of 450,000 Negroes in the South are seriously ill all the time, and that 600,000 of the present population will die of tuberculosis.

The Census shows that both pneumonia and tuberculosis are diseases very fatal to Negroes. And strange as it may now seem, in slavery times Negroes were thought to be practically immune from tuberculosis. Indeed, it is said that, about 1882-3, there was exhibited at a clinic in Charleston, S. C., what was supposed to have been the second case of tuberculosis ever found among Negroes.[12] This is very remarkable, if true.

In each city of the following list of twelve is given the number of times more deaths that oc-

[11] R. W. Woolley, *Pearson's Magazine*, Feb., 1910, p. 210, quoting Drs. Seale, Harris and W. C. Woodward.
[12] Report of *Board* of Prison Inspectors of Alabama, Sept., 1910-1914, p. 45.

curred from tuberculosis among Negroes in 1910, according to the Census, than among whites: Providence, 1.82; Richmond, 2.05; Boston, 2.46; Atlanta, 2.48; New York, 2.64; New Orleans, 2.70; Memphis, 2.80; Philadelphia 3.00; Baltimore, 3.14; Washington, 3.34; Charleston, S. C., 3.55. It may be noticed that more than three and one-half times as many Negroes as whites died of tuberculosis in Charleston. The comparative statistics for pneumonia differ not very much from those of tuberculosis.

However, the ratio of death-rate from combined causes is much lower than this. The average death rate a thousand in eight Northern States in 1910 was 21.9 for Negroes and 15.1 for whites; while the average for two Southern States was 23.7 for Negroes and 15.2 for whites. In ten Northern cities it was 23.64 for Negroes and 15.99 for whites; for the same number of cities in the South it was 30.60 for Negroes and 17.22 for whites.[13] Again, in thirty-three Northern cities the death rate among Negroes was 25.1 a

[13] Northern States: Me., Mass., Mich., N. J., N. Y., O., Pa., and R. I.; Southern: Md. and N. C. These were the only Southern States mentioned in this connection in the census. Northern cities: New Haven, *Boston*, Detroit, Atlantic City, Trenton, Cleveland, Springfield, Philadelphia, Chicago, and Kansas City; Southern: Washington, *Baltimore*, Wilmington, N. C., Mobile Atlanta, Savannah, New Orleans, Memphis, Charleston, S. C., and Richmond.

thousand and 15.7 among whites, while in twenty-four Southern cities the death-rate was 29.6 for Negroes and 16.9 for whites. For the fifty-seven cities together, 27.8 for Negroes and 15.9 for whites.[14] Thus, it is seen that the death rate among Negroes is not far from twice as great as among whites, but contrary to the general impression it is less in the North than in the South.

Moreover, statistics show that the Negro is not increasing in this country as fast in proportion as is the white man. Indeed, he seems to be falling behind in his own percentage of increase. Between 1890 and 1900 his increase was 1,345,318 but from 1900 to 1910 it was only 993,769. Again, the percentage of Negroes in the population of the country decreased from 19.03 per cent in 1810 to 10.69 per cent in 1910, and from 14.13 per cent in 1860 to 10.69 per cent in 1910. In other words, while the whites increased nearly three and one-half (3.4) times between 1860 and 1910, the Negro increased only two and two-tenths (2.2) times.

That this difference between the increase of the two races was not due to the immigration of whites is shown by the fact that from 1800 to 1840 when there was scarcely any immigration of whites the population of the country increased more than

[14] Department of Commerce Bulletin 129, p. 44.

three and a fifth (3.21) times, while from 1870 to
1910, an equal number of years, when immigration was almost at its height, the increase was only
a little more than two and a third (2.38) times.
Again, during the fifty years, 1790 to 1840, it
increased four and a third (4.34) times; also, between 1810 and 1860 it increased in the same ratio
(4.34); while for the fifty years from 1860 to
1910 it increased only something more than two
and three-fourths (2.86) times.

Indeed, it is said that "the Southern States,
which have received practically no immigrants
since the Civil War, have increased their population as rapidly as the Northern States; that is, the
increase of population among the Southern whites
has been equal to the Northern increase assisted
by immigration." [15]

While these facts may not be sufficient evidence
that the Negro will finally become extinct in this
country, nevertheless, it is impossible for one to
escape the conclusion that as the years go by the
members of his race will become fewer and fewer
in proportion to the whole population. As this
comes about the Negro will gradually cease to be
such a problem, as at present.

[15] C. A. Ellwood: "Sociology and Modern Social Problems,"
p. 212.

www.ingramcontent.com/pod-product-compliance
Lightning Source LLC
Chambersburg PA
CBHW050842270326
41930CB00019B/3433